best monologues from the best american short plays

volume three

best monologues from the best american short plays

the best american short plays

volume three

edited by william w. demastes

APPLAUSE THEATRE & CINEMA BOOKS
An Imprint of Hal Leonard Corporation

Published in 2015 by Applause Theatre & Cinema Books
An Imprint of Hal Leonard Corporation
7777 West Bluemound Road
Milwaukee, WI 53213

Trade Book Division Editorial Offices
33 Plymouth St., Montclair, NJ 07042

Printed in the United States of America

Book design by Lynn Bergesen

Library of Congress Cataloging-in-Publication Data

Best Monologues from The Best American Short Plays / edited by William W. Demastes. volumes cm. — (The Applause Acting Series)
    ISBN 978-1-4803-3155-6 (volume 1) — ISBN 978-1-4803-8548-1 (volume 2) — ISBN 978-1-4803-9740-8 (volume 3)
1. Monologues, American. 2. American drama—20th century. 3. American drama—21st century. I. Demastes, William W., editor of compilation.
    PS627.M63B47 2014
    812'.04508—dc23
                        2013041949

www.applausebooks.com

contents

introduction

Speech Acts

"You're fired." "I baptize you in the name of…" "Give me two snow cones." "Those are ugly shoes." "Oh, that this too, too, solid flesh would melt, thaw, resolve itself into a dew." Language is a funny thing, serving humanity in any number of ways by helping us as we struggle to find common cause and establish community in an increasingly crowded but ever alienating world.

Renowned philosopher of language J. L. Austin (1911–1960) spent a career trying to do what most philosophers of language try to do: make sense of human language. He famously popularized the term "speech act," identifying language as something that has performance qualities even though "speech" doesn't actually "act" in any way that we typically describe as "action." It doesn't move things, or touch things, or do much of anything like that. "Stop talking and do something" is a typical response to the perennial advice giver. There's a line between doing and talking that we all pretty much understand. The problem with that common perception, and one that Austin recognized, is that some forms of speech *do* do things that can be called "acts."

Telling someone they're fired certainly has an impact almost as stunning as being hit by a hammer. Declaring someone baptized, or married, or divorced are pretty significant transformative pronouncements, literally converting someone from one kind of person into another. Asking for a snow cone is a gesture that one hopes will lead to a refreshing response, especially on a hot summer day. Criticizing someone's shoes may actually encourage the person to change into something more appealing. These words interact with the physical world and actually have some sort of influence on our surroundings. They're speech acts.

But what about wishing our too, too imperfect bodies would just dissolve and somehow leave nothing behind but the perfection of our souls (in a perfectly idealized world where nothing corrupts or decays)? Is it possible that these opening lines to Hamlet's famous first monologue/soliloquy may actually "do" something? Perhaps it's a perfectly worded sentiment that summarizes exactly how you sometimes feel about this mixed-up, jumbled-up, shook-up world, and it speaks to exactly how you want to deal with it: by simply fading away. Or maybe you never thought about the world in that way at all. Maybe you've been living with some queasy feeling about the world for some time now, but never quite knew what it was you were feeling. Maybe you didn't quite know what it was you were feeling because you never quite knew how to put it into words. Now, however, you've seen your thought perfectly expressed (though Shakespeare's poetic phrasing might not be how *you* would have said this), and now you move forward in life with greater focus because now you know with precision what vague, queasy sentiments had previously been coursing through your veins. "Oh, that this too, too solid flesh would melt" has become for you a transformative speech that gains the name of action by actually altering or focusing what you believe and therefore who you are.

Speech acts. I'm using Shakespeare here because he helps me show what a great phrase "speech acts" is when it comes to describing what happens onstage when actors arrive and find an audience willing to attend to what they have to say. The stage is the space that relies on speech to carry out action. Physical stage actions do occur, of course. People do get into each other's space; they do move about in a choreography of significance. Props are used, and people do interact with them. Physical gestures can make or break an acting style. People touch, gesture, exit. But in the theater it is the language that carries the day. We go for the words.

And when we go to the theater, we go to hear those words spoken by someone, bringing language into direct contact with the physical and engaging the physical before our very eyes. Novels, poetry, the newspaper all have "speech acts" embedded in them, of course. And the streets, our offices, shopping centers, our homes—they are all full of speech acts. But the theater gives us pause to think about these "words, words, words."

"Sticks and stones may break my bones, but words will never hurt me." Really? Words can break spirits, destroy confidence. They can also build hope and incite great acts of heroism. Playwrights know this, and so do theater audiences. Otherwise, why go? How about "what's in a name"? Call a rose skunk weed and maybe it really won't smell as sweet. How easy was it for Romeo to deny his name (or his father)? Romeo he was, and a Montague he remained, despite his naive teenage decision to get out from under the curse of that name. Consequences follow. Words matter and carry clout every bit as dangerous as a hammer or crowbar. This too playwrights know.

The theater, in short, is the laboratory for speech acts. Authors string words together with the complex goal of pulling together disparate audience members into a single attentive community. Even if the goal is to bring everyone together for one single moment of unified laughter, or perhaps a gasp of surprise—even if that small effect is the goal, then the playwright has taken on a pretty daunting and very complex task.

Sometimes playwrights have a political or personal agenda in mind and use the theater to transform an audience's beliefs and attitudes. Is it possible to eliminate or at least minimize such destructive forces as racism, sexism, or nationalism by changing people's beliefs and attendant actions? If so, then speech acts have had their impact.

When it comes to thinking about these transformations, it is generally very difficult to distinguish between conscious and unconscious behavioral shifts. There is little doubt, however, that unconscious shifts have more profound and longer lasting effect. And they are harder to generate as well. So, for instance, walking out of a theater and realizing that Native Americans are a nearly forgotten but still mistreated minority may result in immediate corrective action of one sort or another. We could call that a soft-wiring alteration. But to be exposed in subtle but visceral ways to the persistent, grinding dehumanization that generates discrimination, and to have it somehow sink beneath our consciousness and into our unconscious beings, that's a hard-wire change. How to do these things?

The monologues in this volume are full of speech acts. Some will generate direct action in the form of joyful laughter or the chill of surprise. Others will usher us into worlds we've never experienced, or perhaps into worlds experienced long ago but linger at the furthest edges of memory. Still others may help us alter the way we see certain things, people, or beliefs. I find two works particularly intriguing in this volume. *Deaf Day* by Leslie Ayvazian is a vignette covering a troubling day in the life of a mother dealing with her deaf child. *Struck Dumb* by Jean-Claude van Itallie and Joseph Chaikin presents an aphasic character struggling to regain his control over language. Both remind us of the gift of language. They remind us, in particular, of what we see in all the monologues in this volume: the power and grit of speech acts found in even the "slightest" of pieces. We are reminded by these two works also that speech acts require interaction: speaker and recipient are of equal importance. So do enjoy your read, imagining in your mind's eye exactly how the staged performance might appear.

Best Monologues from The Best American Short Plays, Volume Three, is a collection of monologues drawn from the popular Best American Short Plays series, an archive of works from many of the best playwrights active today. Long or short, serious or not, excerpts or otherwise, this collection abounds in speech acts that may trigger physical reactions and almost certainly will transform an attitude or two, drawing out lost memories, creating new ones, and definitely entertaining, engaging, and amusing us all along the way.

—William W. Demastes
Louisiana State University

best
monologues
from
the best
american
short
plays

volume three

Part I
Monologues for Men

Kimberly La Force

excerpt from

A Marriage Proposal

from

The Best American
Short Plays 2010–2011

MATT   Well, let me start from the beginning. I have been a farmer for years; never too smart but always good with my hands. At first I was a banana farmer in St. Lucia. I had a wife and two young boys and we made good money back then, but the banana industry collapsed when free trade was introduced. [...] Imagine if someone had said that during your testimony, imagine how you would feel. It's okay to listen in church, but then the message goes right out when you leave the church doors. So the demand for our bananas dropped and we were put out of business. Funny thing is that when my money was gone, so was my wife, and I was left with nothing but a field of weeds. I traveled to Texas in 2000 and got small jobs farming there. It was very peaceful, and I harvested for a small canola seed farmer. One day a major company threatened to tell the authorities that my boss was housing illegal immigrants. I was fired and hitchhiked all the way to Florida. [...] So I became invisible, always looking over my shoulder and avoiding the law. I no longer wanted to live life in that way, constantly suspicious of others and always on the move, so I started exploring options. I looked for any loopholes in the law. [...] I tried it all, the temporary visa program, community colleges, lawyers, army recruitments, and churches. They all told me they could help and took my money but gave no results. I even went under an assumed name and worked under the Social Security number of a dead man. For three years I was known as Michael Jones until I was suspected by authorities. I did so much but to no avail, and now I see that the only option for me is to find a wife and her only qualification is that she is a U.S. citizen. [...] I came to you only because after hearing your story, I sensed that you had the maturity to see that marriage is an economic arrangement, not an emotional one. I don't need love from you and I did not come empty-handed. In Texas, the asking price for marriage is about $15,000. I came to you because your problem is financial, and mine is legal. Together we can help each other.

Douglas Soderberg

excerpt from

The Root of Chaos

from

The Best American
Short Plays 1986

scene

The kitchen and dining area of the Cernikowski house in central Pennsylvania.

JOE   [*Father, forty.*] Did it look like a giant woman? [...] It's a family catchphrase. Goes back to your mother's and my courtship. On our first date, I took her to see this movie called *The Attack of the Fifty-Foot Woman*. It was our first date, see, and we were both a little nervous to begin with. We weren't terribly involved in the movie. We weren't scared by it, that is. Well, there came this one part where the mutant title character was, you know, sort of marauding over the countryside. Looking for some mate her own size, I think. You can just imagine why. Anyway, hot on her tail was this sheriff and his goofy deputy sidekick. The infamous tall gal had just terrorized some people parked in a lover's lane, and the sheriff and his deputy come up and ask this teenaged boy and his chippie in a white convertible, "What happened?" Well, the girl is no help at all. She's crying and carrying on and saying, "Oh, it was awful, it was awful!" And the sheriff s asking, "What? What was?" But the girl won't answer. So then the goofy deputy sidekick pipes in with this line: [*Goofy voice.*] "Did it look like a giant woman?" […] Your mom and I just about died. Doublemint, you were conceived later that night. And now, whenever something is really obvious, we say that. A family has got to have catchphrases.

Michael Ross Albert

excerpt from

Starfishes

from

The Best American
Short Plays 2010–2011

setting

A Nova Scotia lighthouse in the late 1980s. The sitting room.

ELI [*Late twenties.*] They're firing lightkeepers all up the coast. It's easier to make these places automatic. Or just get rid of them. It's ridiculous. It, it guides lost vessels back to shore. [Beat.] Anyway, I should go upstairs. [...] When I was younger, I used to listen to other people's conversations on the two-way radio. The lighthouse was so far away from anybody that I... And one day, I heard this girl over the radio. She must've been around my age. Pretty voice. Her name was Margaret, I think. And every Sunday, at the same time, just when I'd be getting home from church, she'd send out the same frequency. [...] I started talking to her over the radio upstairs. There was something about her voice. And I think

I...[...]It felt so...good. To have someone to talk to. Especially after my father died. *Her* father was a sailor. She used to tell me about all the exotic things he brought back with him from his voyages. Ships in a bottle from Martinique, uh...dried-out sea horses from coral reefs. But the thing she talked about most was this starfish. She said it was perfect. She said that God didn't make man in his image. He made starfish instead. [...] The last time I spoke to her, she was going away for the summer. Her father decided to let her travel with him. And...I heard some sailors on the radio talking about it later...Their ship was lost at sea. It must have been a foggy night. Somebody probably forgot to light the lamp in the lighthouse. Excuse me.

Shel Silverstein

excerpt from

The Trio

from

The Best American
Short Plays 1997–1998

setting

An intimate restaurant. DAVID sits at a restaurant table. […]
HELENA sits across from him. Behind them a trio plays—
three women in white dresses.

DAVID   Let me tell you a story—years ago, there was a
cellist—there *was* a cellist—and there still is—I won't state his
name—You'd know it—you—well—he progressed in the
usual fashion—prodigy—Philadelphia—I won't say which
symphony—first chair—and then soloist—He was well
received—well respected. And relatively well paid—*and*
relatively happy—for a while—then what? The pressure—the
celebrity—it started getting to him—not his ego—not his
technique—not his approach—but—something—too much
of something—not enough attention—focus—loneliness? In

any case, he came to me. It was after a performance of
_____. He came to me—"Maestro," he said.
"Maestro, I am…unfit."—*Unfit?* He had performed
brilliantly—or so it seemed to me—what can an outsider see?
Even a conductor—"*In tune with the pulse of each musician*"—
his heartbeat—or hers—

[*She touches his hand.*]

It's a joke—we're not in tune with anything—the instruments
are in tune—the people who bring the instruments to life—I
didn't know what each performance was costing him—what
resources he was calling upon for each—each—what do they
call it on an airplane? A reserve tank? He was running on his
reserve tank. I believe they have them on racing cars—and
what happens to racing cars? Well, he was out—his reserve
tank was out—his wheels were blown out—he was running on
rims—I'm finished, Maestro, he said—I must never attempt
to play again—I laughed a comforting laugh—"Rest," I
said—"I have rested," he answered. "I have rested two
months—since my last concert—and a month before that—
rest is not the answer—I am finished." Well, what did he
need? He was in perfect health—his concentration was
there—the talent…unquestionably—the technique—
impeccable—no personal problems—no drugs—alcohol—
what then?—I said to him, […] step back—not down—do not
step down—step back—"Where?" he said—Back, I said—
back to the comfort, to the family—take a chair—He was not

insulted—he was not shocked—"I don't know if I can even function in a third chair"—Of course you can—step back—He did—I found him a chair in a certain Midwestern symphony—my own group was full—a small, obscure, out-of-the-way—he performed—he supported—he looked to either side of him—he saw friends—he looked straight ahead, he saw someone *else's* behind—ha-ha—sweating—not their behind—they—the soloist—he did *not* sweat—he played—play—that's what we begin doing, isn't it? —We *play* the violin—the *fiddle*—like we *play* hide-and-seek—we *play*—we *play*—and then as we become skilled—the play becomes—*As* we become *brilliant*—ha-ha—the pressure—to *stay* brilliant—to become *more* brilliant—the competition—the success—notoriety—celebrity—the demands of the public—Manolete—the great Spanish bullfighter—he would let the bull come closer and closer to him until after each natural—his suit of lights was slightly torn...closer and closer—he said, "They keep wanting more and I have no more to give." Meaning the public...and the critics—and his own need to...surpass—So he gave the—extra inch—and it was—too much—of course—and this was a poor Gypsy boy who once used to sneak into pastures at midnight—with an old rag—to *play* with the bulls—*play*—You're not playing, Helena—You are performing—admirably—flawlessly—except for the flat of...what?—Joylessness—You are—[...] We can't blame it on love, Helena, love should bring out the best in us—in our art—love should nourish our talent like the rain nourishes a

flower—a seed—springing it to life—to full blazing life—
colors—petals—leaves. […] And you can't compare music to a
flower. Heartbreak can be *heard*—It makes a beautiful
sound—loneliness—it stimulates—practice—we turn to our
instrument—for solace—comfort—no, Helena—love is the
inspiration—unrequited love is the inspiration—loneliness—
pain—think of Beethoven's pain—Satie's pain—Chopin—the
études are written in blood—how many times did Brahms
consider suicide?—daily—moment to moment?—Is suicide
the answer? It's *an* answer—for some—but only the last
answer.

Darren Canady

excerpt from

You're Invited!

from

The Best American
Short Plays 2010–2011

setting

An upscale kitchen in an upscale home.

PAUL   And what is so wrong with being nice? What is so
wrong with a few nice people, getting together, eating some
damn cake, and pretending for just a few hours that they
actually enjoy each other's company? I don't think it's asking
too much for people to put on a happy fucking face, haul out
some manners and good breeding, and do it all in the name of
a four-year-old having a happy goddamned birthday. Pretend,
dammit! Nice people do it all the time. I'm nice—I do it! I
pretend that I want you here, in my house, choking down my
four-hundred-dollar cake and guzzling down the summer
punch I made from mint leaves from my own garden. Because
that's what nice queers do! We invite the half-Jew, half-black

family, and the antisocial single mom to the party because they're oughta be some goddamned solidarity even if you're all raging jackasses and vicious bitches, which I can't tell you you are because I'm the nice one and could a few other people please join me in being fucking nice?!

Mac Wellman

excerpt from

The Sandalwood Box

from

The Best American
Short Plays 1995–1996

setting

In the rain forest of South Brooklyn.

BUS DRIVER   Ever seen a bus before? This is a bus. Don't
just stand there quaking. We in the bus business don't have all
day. We live complex lives. We dream, gamble, seek, deserve
a better fate than Time or Destiny, through the agency of the
Unseen, allows. So get aboard if you are going to. If you dare.
There, there in the valley, someone is playing a saxophone
among the peonies. His heart is broke. There's no poop in his
pizzle, and surely the will of the Unseen shall bear witness
and lift him up from the abyss of his … of his wretchedness, to
the bright air above where lizards, snakes, and the mythic

tortoise are…glub, glub…My basket of sandwiches flew off
into the cheese that is the north end of the thing in the hot
ladder. Groans and slavver. Spit and questions marked on the
margin. A sale of snaps, larval coruscations. Sweet drug of
oblivion. On a global scale. Flowers of unknown radiance,
snarls of snails, all of a coral wonder. Just in time for the man
who discovers himself stubbed, in an ashtray. Put out. All the
work of the Unseen, like a wind in the sail of our hour,
midnight, when we encounter the Adversary, anarchic and
covered with hairs, in the form of our good neighbor's
discarded sofa, left out for the garbage man to pick up. He
would like to discover the truth about what can do no harm
only if it is kept, safely under lock and key, in its cage, with no
poop in its pizzle, aware of us but dimly, us lost in the
crunching despair of our endless opening up before the
doings of the Unseen, in all our sick, sad, pathetic innocence.
Innocence that is only the half-cracked euphemism for our
woe, which possesses not even the required token for the
train, or bus. Nor even the train to the plane. Not even the
faith to enact that pizzle.

Brent Englar

excerpt from

Snowbound

from

The Best American
Short Plays 2010–2011

NOTE:

This monologue may be performed by
either a male or female actor.

time

The present; late January. During a blizzard.

CLIFF [*Late twenties.*] What if in death your soul is
reunited with the souls of those you love—not merely
reunited, but joined. So that by loving another person, and
being loved in return, your spirit—your consciousness—is
enlarged. By loving, you become a more complete person—
and now I'm speaking literally—two souls become one, and
the resulting person, when this soul is reborn— […] The

resulting person carries the accumulated wisdom of two people. And when this person loves and is loved in return, the souls join again, they're reborn— [...] and the resulting person carries the accumulated wisdom of three people, or four, or sixteen, or however many lovers joined in death to create life. So that our purpose in living is to love, and in a perfect world, as we achieve our purpose, we move inexorably toward that moment when every soul that has ever existed is joined together in perfect love. And this is heaven. And this universal soul, bound by love, encompassing all creation, is God. [...] Enforced pain, suffering—call it what you will. When we hurt another person—whether intentional or no, I haven't decided—we lose a piece of our soul. When we die, if on the whole we have hated more than we've loved, we return a less complete person—our soul is less capable of love. [...] What if a person deserved it? What if—the end result is the same. In an imperfect world we move inexorably away from other people until finally each soul is cut off behind an insurmountable barrier. Love is impossible. And this we call hell.

Lisa Soland

excerpt from

Spatial Disorientation

from

The Best American Short Plays 2012-2013

character

JOHN John F. Kennedy Jr., thirty-eight years old, walks with a cane.

time

July 16, 1999, at 8:00 p.m.

place

Essex County Airport in Fairfield Township, N.J.

setting

We are in the terminal of the Essex County Airport, on the night of July 16, 1999, at about 8:00 p.m. The moon has just risen above the horizon but barely casts any light onto the ladder, which can be seen off in the distance, upstage left, representing the steps one must take to board JFK Junior's private plane.

JOHN   You know, everyone thought my father was some great visionary—able to see into the future and claim what human ingenuity could accomplish if we all put our minds to it. After the Bay of Pigs, he conveniently announces that the United States is going to put a man on the moon by the end of the decade, and people are shocked. They think he's nuts. But July of 1969 rolls around and Neil Armstrong places his foot onto the surface of the moon.

[*He rises and crosses downstage, looking out window.*]

That moon. What people don't know is that my father had access to special knowledge that could be obtained by someone like my father, in a family, like my family. He knew that the space program was more than capable of putting a man on the moon when he made that speech in May of '61. He had the information, which made him...powerful really. Powerful. He wasn't so much a visionary as he was a man who knew how to acquire truth. And the truth was what made my father powerful.

James Armstrong

excerpts from

The Rainbow

from

The Best American
Short Plays 2012–2013

time

The present. Labor Day. Around noon.

place

Bryant Park in New York City. There is a picnic blanket spread
on the ground with a knapsack on top of it. Nearby is a metal
table with two chairs.

JACK It's about a lot of things really…Men, and women,
and love, and sex, and jealousy, and the coming together of
people from different parts of the world, and there's
marriages, and struggles, and blasphemy, and faith, and this
teacher who has a really creepy relationship with one of her
students, but then the girl grows up, and all of these people

that you've been following, all these different story lines, they all lead up to this one young woman, and you want, you want so badly for her to find happiness, and there's this guy, and you think, yes, this is it, this is happiness, and everything is finally going to work out, and it doesn't, and it can't, and you know that it can't, so she's left alone at the end, and she looks out over the city, and it's hideous, and it's just sprawling its filth all over, and she looks up, and there's this rainbow. And it doesn't make it all okay. But there's this rainbow. And you think...yes...this...is worth it...Life...is worth it.

• • •

JACK   I had this...relationship. It lasted for a while. And then it didn't. But it was one of those things where...sometimes you spend so much time with one person that...when they're not there anymore...you just don't know what to do. Because sometimes it was really good...and even when it wasn't good...there was still somebody there. But then they're not. Or not as much. And you get lonely. And you realize maybe some of the other relationships in your life...maybe you didn't tend to them as much as you should have. So it was a while ago...but...I guess I'm still getting over her.

Murray Schisgal

excerpt from

The Hysterical Misogynist

from

The Best American
Short Plays 2007–2008

scene

The patio of the East Hampton Golf and Tennis Club. At the rim of the club's outdoor dining area, an isolated, round, white, Formica table with four red-canvassed deck chairs. On the table, a small vase filled with seasonal flowers, a bottle of chardonnay in an iced bucket, a pitcher of water, wine and water glasses, condiments, and the half-eaten remains of lunch. Tennis racquets and containers of tennis balls lie about.

pre-rise sound

Offstage a main-court match is in progress. We hear a tennis ball being whacked back and forth. The crowd of spectators responds with shouts and applause to a well-played volley.

sound

Fades out, gradually, before…

at rise

EMANUEL "MANNY" BROOKS, wearing tennis garb, is slouched in a deck chair, disheartened if not depressed.

time

Summer. Midday.

MANNY   Philip… [*Tormented.*] She called me a misogynist, a man who hates women! She hurled that hideous m-word straight at me, without fanfare, without even telling me what she thought of the play. I was ready to explode!

[*Incredulously.*]

Me, a misogynist? A man who has been married twice, to women! Me, a misogynist? A man who has two grown daughters, both women! Me, a misogynist? A man who adored his mother, a woman! Me, a misogynist? A man who has worshipped women since puberty, a man who has placed women of every conceivable temperament and disposition on a lofty golden pedestal. Me, a misogynist? A man who has loved women, the smell of them, the touch of them, the sight of them, all the days and nights of his life? And not only did I have two wives, two daughters, and a mother, each and every one of them a woman, but I've had dozens and dozens of girlfriends: social girlfriends, professional girlfriends, sleepover girlfriends, live-in girlfriends, engaged girlfriends, married girlfriends, each and every one of them a woman! A woman whom I treated with respect, dignity, and sensitivity! Am I lying? Am I making it up, imagining it? If so, free me from this dark cave of self-deception in which I have imprisoned myself since puberty! [...] Conscience compels me to...Please. Permit me to plead my case. You'd grant that much to a rapist, a pederast, a homophobic. Why not a misogynist, a man who hates women? I have been a working playwright and screenwriter for some thirty years. I've had success and I've had failure. The awards, the applause, and shouts of "Bravo" I received were a verification of my achievements and a faint whisper of immortality. The failures I endured? They were comparable to having a knife thrust and twisted brutally into the arteries of my heart and along with it a burning, raging fever of degradation and humiliation. Equally upsetting is the awareness that, during the course of my career, there have been actors, directors, and producers who have found working with me an unpleasant ordeal. In my defense, let me say that I am not one to place congeniality and camaraderie above the quality of the work that's being done. I am not a pet playwright to be dismissed with a squeeze and a pat on the ass. The quality of the work, at any given moment, is what counts, nothing else, not the company, not the reviews, not the receipts at the box office, not the specious applause of a fawning audience. No one has ever accused me of duplicity. I never put word to paper in order to denigrate and demean a fellow human being or to satisfy a fashionable prejudice. I write not from imagination, but from experience. I write, primarily, to find out what makes me tick as a corporeal being and, yes, to take issue with the sacrosanct conventions of our morally bankrupt society.

[*Vigorously.*]

To be denounced by your wife as a misogynist, which, nowadays, is a battle cry to castigate, to ostracize, to persecute the offender, as the Christian was persecuted during the reign of the Roman emperor Nero, as the Jew was persecuted during the Spanish Inquisition, and as the black man has been persecuted for decades in these United States of America.

[*His voice resonates.*]

I am not...nor have I ever been...a misogynist...a hater of women. I swear on the souls of the women I loved who have passed on and on the heads of my two priceless daughters! [...] Can you imagine the consequences if I, an esteemed playwright and screenwriter, a member of the Dramatists Guild, the Writers Guild, the Actors Studio and the Academy of Motion Picture Arts and Sciences, was publicly accused of being a...a...a misogynist? [...] Do you think I'd be able to raise money to do a play of mine...? Forget Broadway. Forget Off-Broadway. Would I be able to raise money to do a play of mine . . .

[*Stammering.*]

...Off-Off...Off-Off...Off-Off-Off...Off-Off-Off-Off-Off-Off-Broadway?

Craig Pospisil

excerpt from

Dissonance

from

The Best American
Short Plays 2010–2011

setting

A room in a funeral home used for memorial services.

FITZ   [*Mid- to late-forties.*] People misuse the word
harmony. They say it when they mean consonance, where all
the notes complement each other and blend together
smoothly. And consonance is sounds great. But after a while,
it's really boring. There's no tension in music like that.
Nothing to be resolved. Dissonance may not sound pretty,
but it's alive. I always like playing music that moves back and
forth between consonance and dissonance. It means
something's happening. That life is struggling to go on, to lift
itself up.

[*Slight pause.*]

Harmony isn't angelic choirs or perfection. Some of the best harmony has an element of dissonance. It's there, lurking behind the other notes, grounding the piece in reality. I think that's why we like it. It's beautiful, but a little ragged too.

[*Slight pause.*]

Not everything goes. [...] I know what you want me to say. You want me to say I played the piano because I loved it and I loved music, and then you can say, "That's all you need, isn't it?" Well, no, it isn't. I need more. I need to be seen. I need to be recognized. I want my hands back. I want my nerves, my life. I don't want to be working in a fucking funeral home. But this is my life now, so why would I want a goddamn piano?! Like I need another reminder of what a failure I am? What possible use would I have for it?

David Rusiecki

excerpt from

Kid Gloves

from

The Best American
Short Plays 2012-2013

setting

CLAUDIO's desk.

time

The present.

[*We see* CLAUDIO *in his late twenties, in a business outfit, suit and tie, sitting at his desk reviewing papers. A framed photo of a woman and a folder sits on his desk along with a desk calendar, laptop, keyboard, and mouse. An empty chair on the other side of the desk faces him.*]

CLAUDIO   It's Friday, it's payday. I'm good, appreciate you asking. Now, I wanted to start by thanking you for your help this past year. We've seen some significant growth as a department and we're hoping to continue to improve on our system enhancements. We've announced strong results for the fourth quarter and the full year. We improved our performance during the last quarter but we lost some momentum in other areas. Bear in mind, while we are segmented, every area measures their numbers the same way. The process is very similar in the East as it is in the Midwest, to the South region to out here in the West. And, of course, the data we come up with lends itself to things we can update in the future. It all boils down to adaptability. Adapt or die, nothing personal, just business. It's all about change. As you know, change energizes us. You have to embrace change. Not everybody here embraces change. Our employees are naturally stubborn in their ways. I understand, I get it. How's the ancient Chinese proverb go again? "The most consistent thing in life is change . . ." [. . .] Now the key is to follow through with these numbers, continue to improve our processes, find new efficiencies so no details go overlooked, and do our best to try to make us better. My job is to call it out when something isn't working. Why duplicate efforts, you know? Yet at the same time, have employees bring up issues and ideas, provide candid feedback, cut out unnecessary steps, streamline the process, and work together to make sure we're all on the right track. Any questions so far?

Cary Pepper

excerpts from

Come Again, Another Day

from

The Best American
Short Plays 2011–2012

setting

The living room of Ivan Foley, aged forty.

IVAN Goddamn bastards! Stupid pricks! For two months you give 'em your best, while they sit there and sip it through a straw!... Then they narrow it down to you and some other bimbo, and throw you against each other for another month, while they make up their minds... Finally, they name a day when they'll tell you who beat out the other, then they cancel the final interview, say they need more time, and they'll call in an hour! Sure! What do they care! They're safe and secure behind their desks! They've got a job! What do they care about what you're going through!? How many times do they expect you to pour yourself through a tube? How many times do they think you can!?...They'll call in an hour!...Suppose I wasn't here to get the call? Then what?...Would they panic?...Would they sit by their phone all day, dialing and dialing until they got me in? Or would they just call the other guy? "What the hell, one's as good as the other!"...Goddamn, inefficient, inconsiderate, insensitive...

• • •

IVAN   Wait a minute! I see it all now! You are crazy! There never was a contract on me. You're just some street lunatic who picked my apartment at random, and now I'm paying the price! This isn't something that's organized, or paid for. This is just some freaky bit of city madness that's found me...Like the sickos who push people onto subway tracks, or walk down the street hacking up total strangers with meat cleavers...You manage to keep the insanity off you for years and years, and then one day, for no reason at all, out of nowhere, it suddenly finds you...I'm right, aren't I? This whole thing...You're just improvising as you go along. There was no contract...That call was just someone calling to shoot the shit and it turned out to be a lucky dramatic touch. It's all you, right?...I mean, you can tell me. You're still sitting there with the gun.

[*Long pause.*]

John Guare

Blue Monologue

from

The Best American
Short Plays 2007–2008

one of seven works collected by
Daniel Gallant under the heading
Five-Story Walkup

You have to understand Queens. It was never a borough with
its own identity like Brooklyn that people clapped for on quiz
shows if you said you came from there. Brooklyn had been a
city before it became part of New York, so it always had its
own identity. And the Bronx originally had been Jacob
Brock's farm, which at least gives it something personal, and
Staten Island is out there on the way to the sea, and of course,
Manhattan is what people mean when they say New York.

Queens was built in the twenties in that flush of optimism as a
bedroom community for people on their way up who worked
in Manhattan but wanted to pretend they had the better
things in life until the inevitable break came and they could
make the official move to the Scarsdales and the Ryes and the

Greenwiches of their dreams, the payoff that was the
birthright of every American. Queens named its communities
Forest Hills, Kew Gardens, Elmhurst, Woodside, Sunnyside,
Jackson Heights, Corona, Astoria (after the Astors, of all
people). The builders built the apartment houses in mock
Tudor or Gothic or colonial and then named them the
Chateau, the El Dorado, Linsley Hall, the Alhambra. We
lived first in the East Gate, then move to the West Gate, then
to Hampton Court. And the lobbies had Chippendale
furniture and Aztec fireplaces, and the elevators had Roman
numerals on the buttons.

And in the twenties and thirties and forties you'd move there
and move out as soon as you could. Your young married days
were over, the promotions came. The ads in the magazines
were right.

Hallelujah. Queens: a comfortable rest stop, a pleasant rung
on the ladder of success, a promise we were promised in some
secret dream. And isn't Manhattan, each day the skyline
growing denser and more crenellated, always looming up
there in the distance? The elevated subway, the Flushing line,
zooms to it, only fourteen minutes from Grand Central
Station. Everything you could want you'd find right there in
Queens. But the young marrieds become old marrieds, and
the children come, but the promotions, the breaks, don't, and
you're still there in your bedroom community, your life over
the bridge in Manhattan, and the fourteen-minute ride

becomes longer every day. Why didn't I get the breaks? I'm
right here in the heart of the action, in the bedroom
community of the heart of the action, and I live in the El
Dorado Apartments and the main street of Jackson Heights
has Tudor-topped buildings with pizza slices for sale beneath
them and discount radios and discount drugs and discount
records and the Chippendale-paneled elevator in my
apartment is all carved up with Love to Fuck that no amount
of polishing can ever erase. And why do my dreams, which
should be the best part of me, why do my dreams, my wants,
constantly humiliate me? Why don't I get the breaks? What
happened? I'm hip. I'm hep. I'm a New Yorker. The heart of
the action. Just a subway ride to the heart of the action. I want
to be part of that skyline. I want to blend into those lights.
Hey, dreams, I dreamed you. I'm not something you curb a
dog for. New York is where it all is. So why aren't I here?

When I was a kid, I wanted to come from Iowa, from New
Mexico, to make the final break and leave, say, the flatness of
Nebraska and get on that Greyhound and get off that
Greyhound at Port Authority and you wave your cardboard
suitcase at the sky: *I'll lick you yet.* How do you run away to
your dreams when you're already there? I never wanted to be
any place in my life but New York. How do you get there
when you're there? Fourteen minutes on the Flushing line is
a very long distance. And I guess that's what concerns me
more than anything else: humiliation. The cruelty of the

smallest moments in our lives, what we have done to others, what others have done to us. I'm not interested so much in how people survive as in how they avoid humiliation. Chekhov says we must never humiliate one another, and I think avoiding humiliation is the core of tragedy and comedy and probably of our lives.

I went to Saint Joan of Arc Grammar School in Jackson Heights, Queens. The nuns would say, If only we could get to Rome, to have His Holiness touch us, just to see Him, capital H, the Vicar of Christ on Earth—Vicar, V.I.C.A.R., Vicar, in true spelling-bee style. Oh, dear God, help me get to Rome, the capital of Italy, and go to that special little country in the heart of the capital—V.A.T.I.C.A.N. C.I.T.Y.—and touch the Pope. No sisters ever yearned for Moscow the way those sisters and their pupils yearned for Rome. And in 1965 I finally got to Rome. Sister Carmela! Do you hear me? I got here! It's a new Pope, but they're all the same. Sister Benedict! I'm here! And I looked at the Rome papers, and there on the front page was a picture of the Pope. On Queens Boulevard. I got to Rome on the day a Pope left the Vatican to come to New York for the first time to plead to the United Nations for peace in the world, on October 4, 1965. He passed through Queens, because you have to on the way from Kennedy Airport to Manhattan. Like the borough of Queens itself, that's how much effect the Pope's pleas for peace had. The Pope was no loser. Neither was I. We both had big dreams. Lots of possibilities. The Pope was just into more real estate.

My parents wrote me about that day that the Pope came to New York and how thrilled they were, and the letter caught up with me in Cairo because I was hitching from Paris to the Sudan. And I started thinking about my parents and me and why was I in Egypt and what was I doing with my life and what were they doing with theirs, and that's how plays get started. The play I wrote next was autobiographical in the sense that everything in the play happened in one way or another over a period of years, and some of it happened in dreams and some of it could have happened and some of it, luckily, never happened. The play was a blur of many years that pulled together under the umbrella of the Pope's visit.

In 1966 I wrote the first act of this play, and, like some bizarre revenge or disapproval, on the day I finished it my father died. The second act came in a rush after that. But then the steam, the impetus for the play, had gone. I wrote another draft of the second act.

Another: a fourth, a fifth. A sixth. I was lost on the play until 1969 in London, when one night at the National Theatre I saw Laurence Olivier do *Dance of Death* and the next night, still reeling from it, saw him in Charon's production of *A Flea in Her Ear*. The savage intensity of the first blended into the maniacal intensity of the second, and somewhere in my head

Dance of Death became the same play as *A Flea in Her Ear*. Why shouldn't Strindberg and Feydeau get married, at least live together, and my play be their child? I think the only playwriting rule is that you have to learn your craft so that you can put onstage plays you would like to see. So I threw away all the second acts of the play, started in again, and, for the first time, understood what I wanted.

Before I was born, just before, my father wrote a song for my mother:

A stranger's coming to our house. I hope he likes us.
I hope he stays.
I hope he doesn't go away.

I liked them, loved them, stayed too long, and didn't go away. The plays I've written are for them.

Murray Schisgal

Naked Old Man

from

The Best American
Short Plays 2008–2009

NOTE:

Though there's only one speaking part, the cast of
characters is to be published as a program note.

cast of characters

JOSEPH HELLER, novelist, *Catch-22*, etcetera; 1923–1999

ROBERT ALAN AURTHUR, sole producer, co-screenwriter
of *All That Jazz*, etcetera; 1922–1978

ARTHUR KUGELMAN, creative director at advertising
agency; 1928–1999

MURRAY SCHISGAL, playwright, *Luv*, etcetera; 1926–

set

A seven-room apartment on Central Park West. A dining area
adjoining the kitchen: a glossy, square, mahogany table, four
matching, square, ladder-back chairs.

Upstage a long, rectangular, serving table on which we see the following: center, a bowl of fruit; to the right, on a silver tray, two or three large bottles of mineral water and glasses; to the left, several framed family photographs.

time

Spring, early evening, 2009.

[*Lights: Rise and gradually change from natural lighting to artificial lighting. Sound: Softly, Berlioz's "Requiem."*]

[*Offstage, in the foyer, we hear* MURRAY SCHISGAL *speaking in a didactic voice to his wife,* REENE (*pronounced Renee*), *who is getting ready to leave the apartment.*]

MURRAY   [*Offstage.*] Go slow. Take your time. There's no hurry. Don't rush. Be careful. Look where you're walking, especially on the corner of 86th Street. Make sure you look first to the left, then to the right, don't trust the lights, those cars come at you from every direction. And watch where you walk. The sidewalks and gutters are often in disrepair, cracked, caved in. You don't want to trip. You don't want to fall. You don't want to fracture your wrist or your fingers again. Please. Do it for me. And if the bus doesn't come in five minutes, grab a cab. Use your cell phone if you're having any problems. I'll be here. I'll be home. I'll be waiting up for you.

[*Sound: We hear the entrance door open and slam shut. Lights: Rise on dining area as...Sound: Berlioz's "Requiem" fades out.*]

[MURRAY *enters: his hair (possibly a beard) is disheveled. He wears bruised sneakers, khaki trousers, an open-necked, faded, denim shirt, and a maroon cardigan sweater, unbuttoned.*]

[*When seated, he will be at the head of the table, center. Seated from his right to his left are the specters of his grievously missed friends:* ROBERT ALAN AURTHUR, JOSEPH HELLER, *and* ARTHUR KUGELMAN (*aka* BUNNY). *They exist and speak only in* MURRAY'*s imagination (no problem for a playwright).*]

Sorry I'm late. My apologies. Reene usually leaves earlier. But tonight she's having dinner with her friends at Calle Ocho, a South American restaurant on Columbus Avenue. She doesn't have that far to travel. I'm somewhat discombobulated now that you're all here; apprehensive is probably the preferable word. I was afraid you'd think me presumptuous, if not paranoid, in asking you to come visit with me this evening. By the way, if I can get you fellows anything, please speak up.

[*At the serving table,* MURRAY *unscrews the cap and pours himself a glass of mineral water.* JOE *speaks.*]

How many friends is Reene having dinner with? Is that what you asked, Joe?

[*He waits for* JOE'*s assent.*]

Six of them. They play bridge at a midtown club, three, four times a week. It's been terrific for Reene, a lifesaver. It gets her out of the house, keeps her busy, mentally challenged, and happy. I can't tell you how grateful I am to those six women. Not only do they play bridge together, three, four times a week, they also call each other almost every day, meet for lunch, dinner, go shopping, go to Weight Watchers, go to bridge classes, go to the playground to watch their grandkids on the swings and monkey bars until the cows come home.

[*He wipes his brow with a handkerchief.*]

I'll give it to you straight, fellows, I'm envious of Reene for having these six friends. And here's the irony of it.

[*Heatedly.*]

Years ago, I...*I was the one* who had the friends. She didn't have any friends. The friends she had were *my* friends, not her friends. They were all *my* friends. If I wasn't hanging out with you fellows, I was hanging out with friends on whatever play or film I was working on, with friends from Commedie Productions, where, as you know, I was consultant and producer for eighteen years; I also had friends from high school, college, law school, friends from the Actors Studio, the Ensemble Studio, the Writers Guild, the Dramatists Guild, and the Academy of Motion Picture Arts and Sciences!

[*A change of tone.*]

Hey, gimme a break, will you? I had friends up the gazoo. I'm not exaggerating. I had friends I didn't even like, but they were *my* friends nonetheless. I'd estimate I must have had literally hundreds of friends during my lifetime. And they were close friends, not mere acquaintances. We hung out together, spent weekends together, boat trips, vacations... You name it, we did it. But don't ask me what happened to them. I looked around one day and they were gone, disappeared, popped into thin air like bubbles from a bottle of seltzer.

[BOB *speaks.*]

Are you serious, Bob?

[*Laughing.*]

You're asking me how it feels to be an old man?

[BOB *speaks.*]

No, no, I'm not offended. Frankly, I approve your choice of words. I am an old man. You were never one to soft-pedal it. I do miss you. Enormously.

[BOB *speaks.*]

I know where you're coming from, you don't have to apologize. You left us early, at fifty-six, if memory serves.

[BOB *speaks.*]

No, no, it's no imposition. You can't imagine how much I appreciate you fellows coming here this evening.

[*Musingly.*]

Well, let's see, how does it feel to be an old man? To start off with, you wake up one day and you realize that there are countless worlds out there that you somehow missed the first time around.

[*Emphasizing each phrase.*]

Worlds to see...to taste...to touch...to study...to reflect on, to gorge yourself on. I'll paraphrase Tolstoy: Being old is the most adventuresome part of your life. The great man knew of which he spoke, more so than did poor, sad Jacques who described old age as "sans teeth, sans eyes, sans taste, sans everything." Certainly in the early seventeenth century that must have been the case, but certainly not in the early twenty-first century. Frankly, knock wood...

[*He does so.*]

I don't know what it would be like being old without good health. In that regard I've been lucky. A West Coast friend got me started decades ago on a Pritikin diet and a Pilates fitness program. You can't beat the West Coast when it comes to setting the standards for us East Coast slackers; that goes for health, style, cosmetic surgery, and a penchant for multiple liaisons.

[*He drinks, thirstily.*]

After good health, I'd list the necessity to keep busy. Busy with career, with avocation, with hobby, craft, chess, tennis, golf, gardening, with whatever activity engages you, brings a rush of gratification. So far that hasn't been a problem for me. I work every day, seven days a week, writing plays, exclusively. For me, there's nothing more challenging, particularly when writing a play I choose to write, of my own volition, and not for monetary gain. I believe it was Samuel Johnson who said, "No man but a blockhead wrote, except for money." Considering his time and circumstances, I wouldn't argue the point. But writing what one chooses to write? What an exhilarating thought that is. And yet, along with it, a negative thought immediately follows. I do worry about running out of ideas for future plays. When you've been at it for as many years as I have, there aren't that many new ideas loitering about in your imagination waiting for you to explore. Old age, apparently, is a period of reaping, not of planting. Recently, I was encouraged by reading a list of artists who continued to be prolific during their nineties and eighties. Here are a number of them.

[*He gropes through one, two, or three pockets of his cardigan sweater, pants pockets, and shirt pocket for the relevant piece of scrap paper or newspaper/magazine cutout he's searching for. Several pieces of scrap paper, stapled together, catch his eye.*]

This isn't what I was looking for, but I'd like you to hear it. In my opinion, it's the best brief definition of comedy ever written: "If nothing is serious, nothing is funny." That's from the inimitable Oscar Wilde.

[*Glances at the scrap paper behind it.*]

Ah, here's another. It's from Jonathan Swift: "Satire is a sort of glass, wherein beholders do generally discover everybody's face but their own." Not bad, huh?

[*Glances at the scrap paper behind it.*]

And one more: "Comedy is an escape, not from the truth, but from despair." Christopher Fry.

[*He returns stapled scrap papers to pocket, continues searching in his other pockets.*]

Now let me see, where did I put that list…If I had half a brain, I'd file my scrap-paper notes and printed cutouts into the computer. But I'm so damned…Ah, here it is. I have it. On the list of artists continuing to be prolific during their nineties we have:

[*Reads from magazine cutout.*]

"Sophocles, Titian, Bernard Shaw, Somerset Maugham, Jean Sibelius, Frank Lloyd Wright, Louise Bourgeois, Knut Hamsun, P. G. Wodehouse, Oskar Kokoschka," etcetera, etcetera,

etcetera. Prolific in their eighties we have: "Michelangelo, Goya, Tolstoy, Goethe, Wordsworth, Monet, Brancusi, Matisse, Stravinsky, O'Casey," etcetera, etcetera, etcetera.

[JOE *guffaws.* MURRAY *returns cutouts to pocket.*]

You may find it amusing, Joe, but I assure you, my best work lies ahead of me, of that I'm confident.

[JOE *speaks.*]

What was that?

[JOE *speaks.*]

Yes, Joe, I believe the improbable name of Murray Schisgal is right up there with the best of them. That may strike you as a classic case of megalomania, but I am firmly convinced that I have already written plays of lasting significance. Otherwise, I don't see how I could have survived as a writer this long.

[JOE *speaks.*]

[MURRAY *laughing.*]

What? You agree? You don't have to . . .

[MURRAY *laughing.*]

No, stop, I wasn't fishing for . . . You don't have to . . . Stop, that's enough already!

[JOE *speaks*.]

Thank you, Joe. Thank you. That's awfully kind.

[*Nodding.*]

I will. I am. I have no intention of quitting. You have my word on that.

[*He rises, paces around the table and chairs, hands clasped behind his back.*]

Now let's get back to answering your question, Bob: How does it feel to be an old man? Following the prerequisites of good health and keeping busy, I'll add having a few bucks in the bank. Poverty is demoralizing. This from growing up during the Depression. Success and wealth are the primary incentives for a satisfying creative life. This from the '60s, '70s, and early '80s when everything I wrote was produced because of the early kudos I received from the New York critics. My professional decline began in the late '80s, after a few theatrical bombs and a number of perverse screenplays that never got made. I breezed along, nonetheless, primarily on the monies I earned at Commedie Productions as a consultant and producer. Of course, I continued to write plays, many of which were published and produced, both here and abroad; that brings us pretty much up to date.

[*He sits on the upstage rectory table.*]

So far we have good health, keeping busy, and an interest-bearing nest egg in the bank. And here I'm compelled to append a fourth essential ingredient to my recommendations for vigorous aging. Perhaps of even greater value than any of those I already mentioned is being fortunate enough to have at your side a wife, a devoted, affectionate wife-pal, if you will. That's how it goes, fellows. I don't make the rules. And here, once again, I've been a lucky man. It may have worked out in my favor because I married a younger woman.

[BOB *speaks.*]

[MURRAY *grinning.*]

You guessed correctly, Bob. She turned eighty in July. Since I'm eighty-two, she's, by definition, a younger woman. We recently celebrated our fiftieth wedding anniversary. I met Reene when I was twenty-seven and the strangest thing in the world happened when I met her. I felt, for the first time in my life, that I was loved, genuinely, unequivocally, and unconditionally loved. And once I felt that emotion coming from another human being, I was capable of loving another human being. This revelation brought home to me a reality that I had been totally ignorant of. I can only love when I feel I'm being loved. I'm incapable of initiating love. I can only respond to it.

[*He scrounges through his pockets for a handful of scrap paper.*]

I had a thought this morning, just before getting out of bed. That's become a bad habit of mine, jotting down every half-assed idea I have, first thing in the morning. One second.

[*He reads from scrap paper.*]

"Old age is an incomparable high, from which there is no coming down."

[*He looks at scrap paper stapled behind it, then the scrap paper behind that one.*]

By the way, anticipating your arrival, I filled my pockets with some personal notes I wrote on scrap paper and cutouts from newspapers and magazines I've collected these past few years. I thought they might be of interest to you. Listen to these.

[*Reads the first.*]

"Recently a man of ninety-five said to me, 'I've taken a vow of celibacy.'"

[*Waits in vain for a response.*]

Nothing? You don't find it amusing? Okay. Here's another one.

[*Reads the second.*]

"The eighty-one-year-old man shouted in my face: 'You will not rob me of my youth!'"

[*Waits in vain for a response.*]

Still nothing? Anyway, that's how I felt last year.

[*He returns scrap papers to his pocket.*]

Where was I? Oh, yes. I can say, without hesitation, I cherish every single day I'm with my wife. The simple truth of it is that I love her more today than I did yesterday. And I have no doubt I will love her more tomorrow than I do today. Talking about my wife brings to mind a grievance of mine, a decidedly unpleasant aspect of growing old. And for this inexcusable atrocity, I blame, in tandem, Almighty God and evolution. Both are guilty of imprinting, arbitrarily and senselessly, the male genome with the blight of senescent impotency.

[JOE *speaks.*]

You heard me right, Joe, senescent impotency, the inability of a healthy, physically-fit elderly man to have sex with his wife or his girlfriend or his boyfriend or with whomever else he damn pleases! You want to talk about insidious age discrimination, there you have it in a nutshell!

[JOE *speaks.*]

Never mind the argument that senescent impotency is initiated to prevent elderly men from conceiving offspring. I wholly disagree with...

[BOB *interrupts.*]

What was that, Bob? Because they won't be around long enough to raise and protect their offspring? That is such bullshit! How many teenage fathers or fly-by-night fathers are around to raise and protect their offspring? Google the figures and then we'll talk about it. Imagine what it's like living with a woman for fifty years and holding her, kissing her, fondling her, desiring her and... you can't, you're physically incapable of making love to her!

[BOB *speaks.*]

[MURRAY *angrily.*]

Yes, yes, at eighty-two, Bob; to a woman of eighty! Yes, yes, precisely! What is most hateful in all of this is to be forced to keep your hands off your own wife and pretend you're too tired or too old or too preoccupied watching television to indulge in that silly, infantile game of fornication. Bullshit! I'll offer you this platitude: neither Almighty God nor evolution ever had our best interests at heart. They've both proven themselves, again and again, insensitive, indecisive, and totally indifferent to the well-being and happiness of our species!

[*He sits in his chair at the head of the table, empties his glass.* JOE *and* BOB *protest.*]

[*Raising his hands in self-defense.*]

Okay. Okay. I'm sorry. I apologize. I shouldn't have raised my voice. I thought you might like to hear one of the negatives of reaching eighty-two. Let's drop it and get back to the positives. It helps, enormously, if you have devoted children, caring in-laws, and a gaggle of rambunctious grandkids. Granted all those ifs, ands, and buts... Growing old feels pretty damn good and being alive...

[*Grins.*]

feels even better. After much deliberation I've come to the conclusion that luck is a more valuable asset to possess in the long run than talent, wealth, intelligence, breeding, and the personal friendship of the Crown Prince of Saudi Arabia.

[JOE *speaks.*]

Who do I hang out with? That's an easy one to answer, Joe. As I said, except for you fellows, friends of mine are few and far between. Mobility and mortality have taken their toll. More than ever, I find myself hanging out with my wife. It's, frankly, embarrassing for me to always be waiting for her to come home from bridge or from lunch or dinner with her friends or... whatever. I was wondering. Could you fellows possibly come to visit with me once a week on a regular basis? Let's say every Tuesday at 6:30 p.m.?

[*Turns from one to the other.*]

Could you…arrange it? Same time, same place. You needn't stay for more than an hour. Is that possible?

[*He turns from one to the other, waits anxiously to hear a response. They respond positively. Excitedly, beaming, he bangs with fist on table.*]

You agree? It's unanimous? That's great, that is great! I sincerely appreciate it.

[*He rises to refill his glass at serving table.*]

How's it going, Bunny? How are you doing? You've been awfully quiet.

[BUNNY *speaks.*]

How stupid of me! I am sorry.

[*Turns to others.*]

Bob, Joe, my first cousin and my first and best friend of nearly eighty years, Arthur Emanuel Kugelman, better known as Bunny by members of our family. He retired as a creative director at Benton and Bowles a number of years before he…

[*Drops it; turns to* BUNNY.]

Don't be intimidated by these two. They come on like hard-asses, but they're quite harmless. Did you get to hear about

Uncle Hymie? He died last year, one hundred years old.
That's something, huh? I don't know if you've been counting,
but we have three aunts left. Aunt Dora will be one hundred
this year, Aunt Annie ninety-seven, and Aunt Rhoda eighty-
eight. My mother died four years ago at ninety-nine. You
have to admit we inherited a couple of good genes. Even you,
in spite of smoking two packs of cigarettes a day since high
school, lived for seventy-one years.

[*He returns to his chair at table.*]

I remember the day you came into my office at Commedia
Productions. We planned to go out for lunch at Shun Lee
West, chicken chow mein with plenty of crispy noodles, the
way we liked it. I knew you had seen a neurologist that
morning. He had completed a series of tests because you were
having trouble reading. I asked you what he said. "You don't
wanna know," you mumbled, turning away from me. "I do
want to know," I said. And you said, turning toward me, your
expression indecipherable. "I have lung cancer. It's
metastasized to my brain." And then we both turned away
from each other and said nothing...for a minute...for an
hour...for an eternity.

[*A hesitant beat.*]

I was wondering, Bunny, what...what's it been like since
you...?

[BOB *interrupts.*]

[MURRAY *excitedly.*]

All right, all right, I heard you, Bob! What are you getting excited about? I was just going to ask him if...!

[JOE *interrupts.*]

I heard him, Joe. I'm not deaf. You don't have to repeat what Bob said. I get the message. Why are you...? You want me to say it, I'll say it. I am not allowed to talk about what it's like... for the three of you: what you do, what you see, what you feel. It is not permissible.

[JOE *speaks.*]

Fine. Fine. But it seems grossly unfair to me that you can tell me what I can and cannot say when I place no restrictions on what you can or cannot say!

[JOE *speaks.*]

All right, all right, we'll drop it. End of discussion. I'm not wasting the time I have with you fellows on nit-picking technicalities. Now I'd like to tell you something that's totally unrelated to what I was going to ask Bunny. Since it happened to me and not to him, it is permissible. Those are the rules, am I right, Bob?

[*He waits for* BOB *to nod assent.*]

Thank you. We had services for Bunny at the Frank
Campbell Funeral Chapel on Madison Avenue. That was in
1999, the same year you left us, Joe. Anyway, I was asked to
say a few words. Fortunately, I kept a copy of what I said that
morning.

[*Turns to* BUNNY.]

I'd like to read a part of it to you, Bunny. In case you missed
it…the last time.

[*He rises, stands behind his chair as he removes a page from a pants
pocket.*]

I highlighted what I wanted to read somewhere down at the…I
have it.

[*After clearing his throat, he reads from near the bottom of the page.*]

"Bunny was the loudest and the happiest of us all. He loved
his family and he loved being with his family. And as he grew
older and matured and struggled to find his way, he carried
with him a steadfast enthusiasm for family life. Eventually he
found it in a second marriage and in fathering a pair of
priceless daughters, Sarah, named after his mother, and Dana,
named after his brother, David, who was killed on the Anzio
Beach during the Second World War.

[*A beat.*]

"Bunny said two things to me toward the end of his life that haunt me to this day. He said that he was not afraid of death and he said what he resented most about dying was being pitied by others.

[*A beat.*]

"We are not here to pity him or to mourn for him. He lived a full, rich, and fulfilling life. He was and is a brave man; he was and is an irreplaceable friend and a revered member of our family.

[*A beat; without looking at page.*]

"It's not in bad taste to cry when you lose someone you love. If you forgive me my tears, I'll forgive you yours."

[*A beat to collect himself before he returns papers to his pocket and sits at table.*]

[*To* BUNNY.]

Wasn't it in the emergency room at Mount Sinai hospital you said that about dying to me?

[BUNNY *speaks.*]

I'm glad I didn't misquote you.

[*A beat.*]

That brings to mind the time I visited you at the Rusk Institute, Joe. Guillain-Barré syndrome brought you there. You couldn't move your legs, barely move your arms, and it wasn't easy understanding what you were saying. While we were talking, this tall, attractive nurse kept walking in and out of the room, wiping your perspiring face, lifting you up so you could sit properly in bed, taking your temperature and, overall, seeing to it that you were comfortable. None of that surprised me. What did surprise me, though, is when, responding to a gesture of yours, she lifted your body off the bed, seemingly without effort, and carried you to a wheelchair, cradled in her arms as if you weighed no more than a diapered baby.

[*Enjoys the telling of it.*]

And...what was really a shocker, as she...carried you...you turned to me...and you said to me, quite seriously... in that slurry voice of yours: "I'm gonna marry this woman." And you did, you married your nurse, who, at the time, you only knew for a few weeks!

[MURRAY *spontaneously breaks out in laughter; quick to apologize.*]

No offense, Joe. She was a wonderful nurse and turned out to be a wonderful wife, I mean that.

[*Turns.*]

Bob, do you remember when Joe and I went to visit you at New York Hospital?

[BOB *speaks.*]

That's right. You were there for some tests. You thought you'd be getting out in forty-eight hours. Instead, you died before the week was over.

[BUNNY *speaks.*]

You guessed right, Bunny. The same, lung cancer. Kent for you, Lucky Strike for him.

[*A beat.*]

You probably had the easiest time of it, Joe. I heard you went to bed and never woke up from a heart attack. That was quite a memorial they had for you at Ethical Culture. There wasn't an empty seat in the house. Which reminds me, according to the public library, *Catch-22* sold, worldwide, over 10 million copies. It's listed as one of the largest-selling novels of all time. Having you visit with me tonight... It's a special treat for me. I thank you... dearly.

[*Looks to his right.*]

To bring you up to date, Bob... As the sole producer and co-writer with Fosse on *All That Jazz*, you might like to hear that the movie was released a year after you passed away. I know it wasn't anything near the kind of movie you wanted it to be. The good news is that it's become something of a cult favorite and your family probably made some money out of it. Bob Fosse didn't hang around much longer than you did.

[*He drinks some water.*]

But getting back to how it feels being an old man...It's odd, since childhood, I've been blessed and cursed with a rampant imagination. In spite of that, I rarely think about illness and decrepitude. It's as though I haven't the patience for idle speculation. Here's the payoff. Last year, a young woman on the crosstown bus offered me her seat. I was...What? Shocked? Mortified? Humiliated? Yes, all of the above and more. She actually asked *me* if I wanted *her* seat? Can you imagine that? Who...Who asked her to ask me? What provoked her? My demeanor? My posture? My body odor? I took a shower that morning, I shaved (trimmed my beard), I dressed neatly, smartly, I stood straight, shoulders back, chest out, chin tucked in. My mind was reeling. "Please sit down," she said a second time as she stood up. I was furious. I was beside myself. She couldn't possibly think I was incapable of standing on my own two feet! Didn't she realize everyone was staring at me, examining me for possible physical disabilities! I glared at her, venomously, as I shook my head, damning her to the ninth circle of hell for committing the most malicious sin of all: humiliating a...a...a senior citizen...humiliating him in front of a busload full of strangers!

[A beat to collect himself.]

I've reached the conclusion that being old can be defined as being naked. Every effort to conceal your aging from others has been in vain. Like King Lear, you're constrained to flaunt your naked self, your shriveled, desiccated, mortal self, so that you, too, can see with your eyes...what others see with their eyes...a poor, forked, naked old man as thou art.

[A beat.]

Friendship now requires that I introduce to you a dimension of my self that is *not* visible. I haven't told this to anyone, not even Reene. Frankly, I'm not even sure I'll ever tell her. I have no idea how she'll react, and I don't, above all else, I don't want to cause her any unnecessary heartache.

[He sits on serving table, clasping his hands on lap; ruminates.]

I was fifteen, employed as an after-school usher at the Loews Premier on Sutter Avenue, when I broke with my orthodox heritage. It was Passover and while at work, after much deliberation, I walked up to the candy counter and bought a Hershey bar with almonds. You should know, Bob, that during the Passover holiday you're only allowed to eat foods prepared for Passover on a separate set of dishes. Hershey bars with almonds were definitely forbidden. Nonetheless I ate the candy bar, seated in the last row of the balcony, watching a movie. Gradually I stopped going to religious services on a regular basis; from there on I was on the bumpy road to perdition. In spite of that, in times of dire stress, I prayed to God, asking for His help in solving one dilemma or another. I did see to it that my children were bar and bas mitzvahed and that my grandkids called me Zada. As a gesture of Jewish solidarity, I belonged to one synagogue or another, which I attended three times a year for the High Holy Days. Later on, much later on, when I was in my seventies, without any discernible cause except, perhaps, excessive anxiety, I started praying every morning, staring out of the living-room window as the sun rose in the east.

[*He rises, stands behind his chair, and prays, eyes closed, hands clasped, head bobbing back and forth, earnestly, quietly.*]

"Chamois Yisroale adonoi aliena, Adonei he Chad. Baruch hem recall melaena l'oilom voyed. Hear, oh, Israel, the Lord is my God, the Lord is one. Blessed be his glorious kingdom for ever and ever. You shall love the Lord your God with all your mind, with all your strength, with all your being. Set these words I command you this day upon your heart. Teach them faithfully to your children; speak of them in your home and on your way, when you lie down and when you rise up. Bind them as a sign upon your hand; let them be a symbol before your eyes; inscribe them on the doorposts of your house and on your gates. Be mindful of all my mitzvoth and do them: so shall you consecrate yourselves to your God. I, the Lord, am your God, who led you out of Egypt to be your God; I, the Lord, am your God.

[*He opens his eyes, unclasps hands.*]

So I prayed, until recently, every morning at sunrise. I prayed for the recovery of people I loved who were dying. I prayed that the war in Israel would end. I prayed that the ice caps on the North Pole would stop melting. I prayed that a play of mine opening that evening would receive favorable reviews, etcetera, etcetera, etcetera. My naivety embarrasses me. I'm certain there's a simple theological explanation why my prayers went unanswered. But, obviously, throughout the millennia, billions of people have prayed billions of times, and if their prayers had been answered, there would have been and there would be today billions of healthy, wealthy, happy, peace-loving people. And we know none of that ever happened. We can logically assume, putting aside statistical probabilities, that their prayers went unanswered. And yet, by the billions, people continue to pray. Admittedly, there is in prayer itself an indefinable sense of consolation, of reassurance, of somebody up there really cares about me. So I, too, continued praying. I was touching all the bases and doing harm to no one. Pascal knew of what he spoke. There are no losses in the game of prayer.

[*Seated at table.*]

Once again, this was until recently. Now, I no longer get up to pray as the sun rises in the east. I no longer go to a synagogue three times a year for the High Holy Days. And, frankly, I feel better with myself for it, no more than that; I feel better with myself for it.

[*He scrounges through his pockets until he finds the cutout he's looking for.*]

Charles Kingsley, a nineteenth-century minister, wrote a letter to T. H. Huxley, offering his condolences on the sudden death of Huxley's four-year-old son. In his letter Kingsley stated that if Huxley would open his heart to God's promise of eternal life, he could look forward to meeting his son in heaven. This is Huxley's reply.

[*Reads.*]

"I cannot sufficiently thank you...My convictions...on all the matters of which you speak, are...firmly rooted. But the great blow which fell upon me seemed to stir them from their foundation, and had I lived a couple of centuries earlier I could have fancied a devil scoffing at me...and asking me what profit it was to have stripped myself of the hopes and consolations of the mass of mankind? To which my only reply was and is...Oh, devil! The truth is better than much profit. I have searched over the grounds of my belief and if wife and child and name and fame were all to be lost to me one after the other as the penalty, still I will not lie!"

[*He returns scrap paper to pocket.*]

Anyway, you may well ask: Why did I make the choice not to pray? Why recently? Why not sooner, earlier? Let me shed myself of all duplicity. At my age I refuse to speak to someone who refuses to speak to me. Furthermore, I amnot here on this wobbly patch of earth to be swayed from what I perceive to be reality. To paraphrase Bertrand Russell: There's something contemptible about a man who can't face the dangers of life without the help of comfortable myths.

[*A beat.*]

What I failed to say previously in listing for you the good fortune I've had, my health, my marriage, children, grandkids, having the time to write and read what I choose...What I didn't tell you, what I couldn't tell you, is that there is, with aging, the oppressive burden of mortality. You can see it in the texture of your skin when you shower, you can feel it when you run your finger over the bulging blue veins on the back of your hand, you can taste it before you have breakfast in the morning. Yes, taste it. This from Montaigne, my incomparable mentor: "So I have formed the habit of having death continually present, not merely in my imagination, but in my mouth." So it is that I taste it before I have breakfast in the morning. And, finally, you can sense mortality in the uncertainty of your stride when you start off on your daily walk and you can smell the stench of mortality before you fall asleep at night.

[*Bitterly.*]

For this abomination, I fault Almighty God and the forces of evolution. They and they alone are responsible for severely limiting the lifespan of humankind. Almighty God, in a brief fit of distemper, "Dust you are and to dust you shall return," cursed Adam and Eve because Eve was eating an apple. Afterwards, he arrived at the paltry figure of 120 years. At the other end of the spectrum, evolution, without a thought in its empty head, decreed that humankind will live for an indeterminate age, hop-scotching from twenty years in medieval times, to forty-five years at the beginning of the twentieth century, to seventy-eight years at the beginning of the twenty-first century, thanks due to the revelations of medical science.

[*A note of desperation.*]

I ask you, why did God and evolution choose such paltry longevity numbers for their ostensibly preferred species? There are tortoises that live over 150 years, whales that live over 200 years, and Icelandic clams that live over 400 years! What are we, orphans, rejects, biologically inferior to the Icelandic calms? Hey, gimme a break, will you?

[*He scrounges through his pockets until he finds the piece of scrap paper he's looking for.*]

I have something here that gets into what I'm trying to...Listen to this.

[Reads from scrap of paper.]

"Over 99 percent of the species that ever walked, flew, or slithered upon this earth are now extinct. When we look at the natural world, we see extraordinary complexity, but we do not see optimal design. We see redundancy, regression, and unnecessary complications; we see bewildering inefficiencies that result in suffering and death." That's from Sam Harris's *Letters to a Christian Nation.*

[He returns scrap paper to pocket.]

So where does this leave us? It leaves us between a rock and a hard place, between a mute, tyrannical God and the blind, blundering force of evolution, both of whom are responsible for a failure of "optimal design" and "bewildering inefficiencies that result in suffering and death." No doubt the average lifespan for humanity will continue to increase at a snail's pace, once again, thanks due to the revelations of medical science.

[MURRAY sits at the table, visibly distraught. He looks at each of his guests, speaks softly.]

I have a...an embarrassing confession to make...to each of you. For the last year or so, I've been taking pills to get through the night. I find it increasingly difficult to forget that I'm eighty-two years of age, shorn of my youth, my vigor, my sexuality. My cache of good fortune seems to have petered out. More and more I find myself counting the hours left in a day, the days left in a week, the weeks left in a year. I listen with dumb fascination to the beating of my heart, the throbbing of my pulse, the scuffling of my footsteps. At times, a scream of hopelessness congeals in my throat, a burgeoning, suffocating scream.

[*In a strangled voice.*]

I can barely breathe. I stretch my mouth wide open and I try to scream...with all my might, with every muscle in my throat, my face, my lungs.

[*He opens his mouth as wide as he can, tilting his head upwards, but the only sound he emits is a barely audible, pitifully plaintive moan.*]

Ahhh! Ahhh! Ahhh! Ahhh!

[*Frustrated, he gives it up.*]

But there is, I discovered, no scream in me; no release; no reprieve. I gasp. My eyes see double. My body trembles. My ears ache with the piercing sound of some hellish fiend... howling and screaming...in...in the cave of my skull... and...and all of a sudden...it occurs to me...to pray.

[*A breath of relief.*]

To Almighty God. To pray. To ask for help. Why have I wasted all this time? How could I be so blind, so stupid? I must pray. I must ask for his forgiveness, for his absolution, for his blessings so that I may live to see the sun rising once again in the east.

[He jumps to his feet, stands behind his chair, and prays, eyes closed, hands clasped, head bobbing back and forth, loudly, frantically.]

"Chamois Yisroale adonoi aliena, Adonei he Chad. Baruch chem mecall melaena l'oilom voyed. Hear, oh, Israel, the Lord is my God, the Lord is one. Blessed be his glorious kingdom for ever and ever. You shall love the Lord your God with all your mind, with all your strength, with all your being. Set these words I command you this day upon your heart. Teach them faithfully to your children; speak of them in your home and on your way, when you lie down and when you rise up. Bind them as a sign upon your hand; let them be a symbol before your eyes; inscribe them on the doorposts of your house and on your gates. Be mindful of all my mitzvoth and do them: so shall you consecrate yourselves to your God. I, the Lord, am your God, who led you out of Egypt to be your God; I, the Lord, am your God.

[In a panic, MURRAY interrupts the above prayer, whenever reflection supersedes impulse.]

But then I think: What in the world am I doing? Am I going crazy? I don't believe in an Almighty God! I'm a non-believer, a secular Jew who recognizes and acknowledges that only through the genius of medical science can we look forward to living 100, 200, 400 years, like the Icelandic clam! What am I carrying on about? Nothing I do or say will change anything. I'm your run-of-the-mill naked old man, scrounging about in the dustbin of time.

[*Talking to himself.*]

The jig's up. The party's over. The days grow short when you reach September. If that's all there is, my friend, then let's keep rocking and bring down the . . .

[MURRAY *hears something in the hallway. He jerks his head to listen. Sound: The offstage entrance door opens and slams shut.*]

[MURRAY *whispers; frightened.*]

It's Reene. She's back. She's home.

[*Glances at his wristwatch.*]

It's too early. Something must have happened. Maybe she fell, hurt herself, broke her wrist or fingers or . . .

[MURRAY*'s three spectral guests rise and exit, downstage right. Follows them but doesn't exit, still whispering.*]

Where are you guys going? Why are you leaving? We haven't finished. We still have a lot to . . .

[*A beat.*]

Are you coming next Tuesday? You promised, 6:30 p.m.
Don't forget. I'll be waiting for you!

[*He hurries to exit the dining area, upstage left.*]

Reene? Reene? Where are you? Why did you come back so
early?

[*He searches for* REENE *throughout the apartment, his voice receding further and further away from us.*]

[MURRAY *offstage.*]

Is everything all right? Did anything happen? You didn't fall
and hurt yourself, did you? Are you ill? Do you have a
headache? Is your hip bothering you? Your sinuses? I'll heat
up a cup of English Breakfast tea with lemon. How was
dinner? Did you enjoy yourself? Was it fun? Where are you?
Reene? Reene? Where did you go to? Will you answer me? Is
anything wrong? Will you do me a favor and answer me?

[*Sound:* MURRAY's *voice fades out as...Lights: simultaneously fade out.*]

John Guare

What It Was Like

from

The Best American
Short Plays 2009–2010

one of seven works collected by
Daniel Gallant under the heading
Seven Card Draw

character

NARRATOR, male, late twenties–early forties

Happiness. I had met the woman who'd become my wife on
Nantucket in 1975 and it looked as if Adele and I might
actually work out, or, more to the point, that I might not
mess it up. I was finally living in my future. One day while
walking along Hudson Street in Greenwich Village, where I
lived, a flash of yellow crashed into me. A spandex-clad cyclist
leaned over my body, sprawled on the pavement, and yelled
down at me, "You broke the chain on my ten-speed Raleigh!
You broke the chain on my ten-speed Raleigh bike! I wish you
were dead! Die! Die! Are you dead?" He went off, pushing his

lopsided yellow racer, screaming, "Die! Die!" I limped home. Nothing had happened, but suppose I had died? Worse— suppose something had happened to Adele? What would happen if I lost all this? How permanent was this unusual, precious happiness that she had brought to my life? What was the shelf life of our time together? I suddenly could imagine dying. The unimaginable became imaginable. But if I lost everything, what would I be left with? Everything seemed to be so perilous, life merely waiting to be broken by a yellow spandex flash out of nowhere. Is it all Mary Tyrone's last line in O'Neill's *Long Day's Journey Into Night*: "And then I...was so happy for a time"? Things in the seventies were not so hot for little old New York. Like me and that cyclist, the city constantly careened on the brink of collapse. Basic services vanished. Garbage seemed to collect everywhere on the street. Gangs of thugs would set those piles of trash on fire. Lots of street crime. People exchanging mugging stories became the new small talk. "I gave him all I had. He waved his gun at me: 'Is this it?'" "Would you take a check?" Graffiti tattooed walls, windows, buses, billboards, parks. An English friend said the graffiti made each subway train zoom into the station with the force of an obscene phone call. On October 30, 1975, the *New York Daily News* headline immortalized President Gerald Ford's response to this blight: FORD TO CITY: DROP DEAD. A massive, oppressive construction called the West Side Highway ran above and along the abandoned rotting piers that lined the Hudson River on West

Street from Christopher Street to Fourteenth Street. In the round-the-clock darkness under the highway, trucks were parked, block after block of trucks, their rear doors hanging open, inviting anyone who desired to climb in, turning this underbelly into an ulcerous parking lot from hell. A sub-subculture of illicit sex, drugs, violence festered in the backs of these trucks. Were they abandoned? Where did they come from? You would never walk along the river at night unless you were feeling suicidal. Don't forget the unsolved Greenwich Village "bag murders"; butchered bodies in black plastic bags would float in the Hudson right off this hellhole. And just to keep you on your toes: a gang of wild neighborhood kids went around beating up people at random. Yet I was the happiest I'd ever been in my life. When I met Adele in 1975, I was living in the Village near the river on Bank Street in what had been John Lennon's apartment before he moved uptown to meet his fate in the Dakota. What an apartment! It consisted of two rooms, the first being the ground-floor length of the brownstone building, windowless and very dark; the second room was all light, a thirty-foot ceiling, banks of skylights, a spiral staircase leading to the roof garden. An unnamed sculptor decades before had built this dream studio on what had been the brownstone's garden. Part of me loved living in the shabby residue of John Lennon's fame. It made me interesting. Another part of me refused to face the fact that the apartment was unlivable. The studio room with the thirty-foot ceilings and skylights was impossible to heat in the winter. The drinks by my bed would freeze during a January night. In the summer it would take a nuclear-powered AC to cool this thirty-foot-high inferno. I asked the landlord, "Why did John Lennon move out?" "He wanted more room." And I said, "But that's why I'm moving in." The rent for the time was outrageous. Five hundred dollars a month. I took it. All that remained of John and Yoko was a large bed in the center of the room with a number of posts around it; attached to each post was a television set tuned to one channel. In pre-cable days this meant seven TVs, seven stations. My predecessors apparently would stay in bed wearing headsets whose sound channels they would switch as they switched (or didn't switch) their eyes. The first night I moved in I heard scratching at the front door, which led up a short flight of stairs onto the street. "John," the voice said. "Who is it?" I asked brightly as I started to unlock the door, sure it was some pal stopping by to see my new glamour pad. The desperate voice mewled, "John, let me in. I've come such a long way." Which friend was playing a joke? "No, who is it?" "John, let me in, I love you." "Tell me who you are." " John, I love you. Let me in." The creepy urgency in the late-night voice was no joke. I didn't open the door. The scratching and weeping continued all night. I opened the door in the morning. Bouquets of wilted flowers lined the doorstep with a card: "I love you, John." Almost every day in the four years I lived there I would find sprays of roses or chrysanthemums left at the door or elaborately decorated cakes with "John Forever" in frosting or long, yearning confessional letters that only John—the other John, the real John—would understand. They told me their secrets. In those pre-Internet days, these pilgrims had not yet learned that the object of their obsession had moved uptown; 105 and one-fourth Bank Street (yes, one-fourth, not one-half) was still the requisite destination for their hajj. I'd say to the anguished spiritual travelers huddling outside my door, "He doesn't live here." "But we've comes so far. Australia. Japan. New Zealand. Oregon. Germany. Where is he?" Sometimes they'd get very angry. "Hey, don't get mad at me, I'm not hiding him. He doesn't live here. I swear to you. Yoko doesn't live here. No, I don't know where he went. Back off." "Let us in." "No, you can't come in." "We want peace!" "I want peace!" "We have to come in!" I understood that. I wanted "in" somewhere as well. I wanted peace as well. What was my life going to be? I inadvertently lived in a world that for so many others was the Mecca of desperate dreams. Why couldn't I be that John? Once, someone left a delicately painted, self-proclaimed official passport ensuring John free passage to anywhere in the universe. Why couldn't I have a passport like that to get me out of that place Wallace Stevens described so accurately, where one's desire is too difficult to tell from despair. I had a baby grand piano I loved to play, gleefully torturing my next-door neighbors John Cage and Merce Cunningham, who would pound on the wall for me to shut up. I'd leave my apartment, size up today's crowd of

Lennonites, and then I'd trot up the street to do my day's errands—and watch out for yellow bikes. And then in the midst of all this, I met Adele. My next play came together out of incredible happiness and daily violence and insatiable yearning in this failing city that dreamed of success. Sometimes happiness gives you the security you need to go into the dark places. People always lament what the city used to be, or what a neighborhood once was. That's what I love about New York City—it's always being reborn, it's always reinventing itself. And it demands the same of you—that you keep readjusting to time. You can't live in the past in this city; it's just not there anymore.

Lawrence Thelen

Ichabod Crane Tells All

from

The Best American
Short Plays 2011–2012

character

ICHABOD CRANE

scene

A lecture on stage, 1840.

synopsis

In this comic one-man play, Ichabod Crane, at the very old age of seventy-two, gives a lecture concerning the events which led to his departure from the small town of Sleepy Hollow fifty years earlier.

to the actor

It's worth noting that nearly everything Ichabod says about his time in Sleepy Hollow is a lie—devised over the years to make himself look better in his stories and justify his actions. He might even believe these lies to be true, forgetting long ago how the actual events played out. Despite what he says, the truth is: he was *very much* in love with Katrina Van Tassel, *terribly* jealous of Brom Bones, and *scared to death* of the Headless Horseman. Yet, over the years, he has created another reality to counter the stories that flowed forth following the events that suggested he was overly timid, a failed lover, or even insane. It would be invaluable to communicate some of this to the audience.

[*As the house lights dim, a spot light comes up on a lectern center stage. ICHABOD CRANE walks to the lectern and addresses the audience. ICHABOD is a spry, feisty, seventy-two-year-old man. He is tall, thin, lanky, and out of proportion—looking more like a Harlequin marionette whose head is too big for the rest of his body, and whose ears and nose are too big for his head. His arms and legs are longer than they should be and don't always seem to move with the same goal in mind. He has gray hair and a sage, serious expression, which becomes almost sinister when he smiles. He is a blindly arrogant man who does a very poor job of masking his disdain for the ignorant and stupid people of the world. Yet he likes himself an awful lot.*]

ICHABOD CRANE   Good evening. I'm Ichabod Crane, and it's a pleasure to be here. I've been asked to give a lecture on the circumstances surrounding my time spent in that dreary little New York town of Sleepy Hollow, and the events that led to my departure—a story which seems to have become "legend" over the years. I appreciate the Library Association and the Town Council for asking me here so I can finally tell *my* side of the story; for many misrepresentations and rumors have been spread over the years—particularly by that most unscrupulous journalist Washington Irving—and other cynical writers who have grossly misinterpreted my character for years. Now, let me state from the outset that there was, and to the best of my knowledge, still *is* a Headless Horseman who roams the village of which I speak, and that he was in no way an apparition, a hoax, or a bit of indigestion as some have suggested.

Several have said that my timidity, my belief in the supernatural, or my failed marriage proposal to Miss Katrina Van Tassel, led to a temporary insanity—a swelling of the brain twice the normal size—which led to hallucinations conjuring up this Horseman. Well, that's simply preposterous! If my brain had swelled to such proportions, it would have exploded along the roadside like a shattered jack-o'-lantern.

Let me start by going through each of those points with you one by one so there's no misunderstanding. First of all, I am not a timid man. In fact, I'm quite gay, fun loving, and gleeful. I can be raucously funny at times. And I'm quite wonderful at a party, for I can speak to nearly anyone on nearly any subject even if the person to whom I'm speaking bores me to death. I've learned to conceal my disdain very well over the years. It's all in the smile.

[He smiles.]

No one can be unhappy when they're looking at this face. Secondly, as far as my belief in the unknown goes—the supernatural, superstition, coincidence, and all that—it is true I believe in such things, for I have experienced them firsthand—irrespective of that ridiculous Headless Horseman event. I have seen and heard things that no man has seen or heard. Yet, that doesn't make me insane—as some have suggested—but rather *exceedingly* sane. More sane than any of you. What's more, if anyone here tonight can prove to me in facts and figures that the supernatural *does not* exist, then let him speak now or forever hold his tongue. No! I am speaking now. You can speak later!

[He regains his composure.]

Finally, as far as Miss Van Tassel goes, it wasn't a failed marriage proposal at all. How do these rumors get started? I never had any intention of proposing marriage to the girl. It's true that she was enamored with me, and that we spent nearly every weekend together while I was in town, and that many *assumed* I would propose to her—but the whole thing is one big misunderstanding. In the end—and let me be perfectly clear about this—it was *I* who rejected *her*, not vice versa. I have not been rejected by a woman one time in my life. Ultimately, you see, Miss Van Tassel was not my type of woman. Her table manners, for example, were atrocious. I once spent a whole evening with her during which she had a pea stuck between two teeth the entire time.

And for those of you who might believe that my real interest in the girl lay not with *her*, but with her father's well-stocked bank accounts, that too is false. True, it would have been nice not to have to confine myself to a classroom for fifty years teaching retched little monsters the basics of modern-day survival just to earn a living. But I couldn't bear the thought of returning home each evening after a long day's work to that sour expression with which she often greeted me. Not even for a sizable inheritance. Everyone has their limits, and Katrina Van Tassel was mine.

[*He takes a moment to gather his thoughts.*]

Let me start at the beginning. One day back in 1790, as a young lad of twenty-two, I came across a posting in the local newspaper for a schoolmaster. I'd had no formal training for such a position, but I'm naturally bright—as I'm sure you can tell—and had self-taught myself most everything a person needs to be successful in life. I've always been very well read, having gone through Milton and Shakespeare and even the Bible—a ghastly piece of propaganda which, surprisingly, turned out to be quite useful in the classroom when it came to questions I didn't want to answer: "Where is the universe, Mr. Crane?"—"Read your Bible!" "Why is my uncle also my father?"—"Read your Bible!" "Where does snot come from?" Well, some questions even the Bible can't answer.

Let me, if I may, interject here my teaching philosophy for those teachers in the audience who will no doubt want to emulate me. First of all, don't give the little brats an inch or they'll walk all over you. Children must have discipline. Discipline and boundaries.

They must know what they *can* do and what they *can't* do. Otherwise, they'll waste all their time—and yours—testing the boundaries and not thriving within the established structure. Now, the best way to organize this structure, I have found, is around pain. When they do what you want, you say, "good Johnny," or "good Sally." But if they are wrong, or bad, or disgusting, pain will rectify the situation immediately. If they miss a math problem, for instance, a wrap on the knuckles with a ruler will suffice. For more grievous acts such as spitting or smoking, I've found a good smack across the face will instantly change that behavior. And on it goes from there. It should be noted that, to date, none of my students have ever died in the classroom. I'm simply doing a parent's job. Why anyone in the world would want to have children in the first place is beyond me—but as long as they're around, it seemed like educating them would be a sensible way to make a living.

At any rate, I answered the newspaper ad because it seemed like a good time to leave Connecticut, where I was born and raised. I had been working as a stock room manager at Anderson's Livestock, Lumber and Feed Store for six months, and had quite a good relationship with Mr. Anderson and his daughter, Sonia, who naturally acquired a crush on me. But the dust and the hay played havoc with my sinus, and manual labor was of no interest to me whatsoever. I've always been far more interested in using my brain than any other part of my body. And when I explained this to Sonia, her goodwill towards me went elsewhere—and, consequently, so did I.

Luckily for me, the very next day I received a letter from Baltus Van Tassel, head of the Sleepy Hollow school board and father of the aforementioned Katrina Van Tassel—the girl with the pea in her teeth. The letter included a one-year school master's contract—commencing at two dollars a week—and a one-way stagecoach ticket to get there. What a horrid way to travel—my bony little bum was sore for a week. Nevertheless, I accepted the position immediately; not because I *needed* the job, but because I was horrified at the thought of so many uneducated New Yorkers being set loose on society.

When I arrived in Sleepy Hollow it was clear the town desperately needed me. The previous schoolmaster had failed miserably as far as I could tell. The boys were working in the fields getting their hands abhorrently muddy, and the girls were learning cooking and cleaning from their mothers. They clearly had no desire to better themselves. So I took it upon myself to do that for them.

No room and board was provided with the position, so I was taken in by the families of those I taught—I rotated weekly from house to house. Needless to say, some accommodations were worse than others. One home, for example—that of the Mullet family—was particularly gruesome. I was provided with a flea-infested cot in a dank and dirty cellar—no closet, no bureau, not even a mirror with which to perform my ablutions. Hell, everyone deserves a mirror. And my meals consisted of soup. Every day another soup: cabbage soup, parsnip soup, boiled celery soup—God forbid they should toss me a bit of meat once in a while. I'm not a glutton, but I've always had a healthy appetite. I swear I lost five pounds the week I stayed with the Mullets. Needless to say, I never went back there again.

By contrast, there was the home of Darius Vanderhoff. Now, the boy, Darius, was a lost cause—a true dirt clod—but his mother provided me with the heartiest meals I received during my tenure. Lamb stew, chicken and dumplings, pot roast. Gravy has always been one of my favorite indulgences, and Mrs. Vanderhoff knew her way around a smooth sauce. What's more, I was provided a bed in their kitchen, where many a night a second supper was to be found amid the cupboards and icebox. Mrs. Vanderhoff chalked up the lost food to a mother raccoon she had seen seeking nibbles for her young. Not wanting to spoil her feeling of goodwill toward animals, I continued to let her believe such a wild story. Through a fine bit of finagling, I was able to reside at the Vanderhoff's home on four separate occasions. I tried for a fifth but their bankruptcy prevented it. Clearly, the nicest home I was privy to was that of the aforementioned Baltus Van Tassel—father of the daughter with the pea?—who was clearly the wealthiest man in town. There I was given my own private room—with a mirror—and three filling, though flavorless, meals a day. Mrs. Van Tassel was not what you might refer to as a gourmet. Still, I never went hungry. Their youngest daughter, Mildred, was one of my students—and upon my first stay Mildred introduced me to her older sister, Katrina, a bouncy young woman of eighteen. It was obvious that Katrina was taken with me immediately. I saw it coming but there was nothing I could do to prevent it. I say this with all due modesty. She fawned over me the same way a squirrel fawns over a nut.

And I must say I liked it very much. So, I indulged her infatuation by staying at their home as often as possible, and visiting her on weekends as well. And each time I stayed I received more attention from her than the previous visit. Which only stands to reason; we were getting to know one another better with each passing day. As one would expect, a romance developed.

[*He smiles grandly, showing he is quite proud of this feat.*]

Or, at least, that's what I let her believe. I let her indulge her fantasy with me though I was not smitten with her at all. Oh, yes, she was beautiful, with a slim, tight little body, and a sensual, erotic smile, and all the money in the world. But she really wasn't my type. And the stories that state that my lip quivered whenever she came near me, or that I had to sit down every time she took my arm are blatantly false!

I was soon to discover, however, that there was another man interested in Katrina—Abraham Van Brunt, also known as Brom Bones. I assume he acquired the nickname because of his large, unwieldy physical resemblance to a pachyderm. Nonetheless, Miss Van Tassel had apparently had a previous, albeit short, courtship with the large fellow; and although I know not the reason for their separation, it was clear she had no interest in resuming the courtship with him once I came along. In fact, often in his presence, she would dote on me even more than usual—presumably to show him what a better catch I was, or to keep his feelings for her at bay.

Now, that's not to say they were *complete* enemies. I did happen upon them once in the pantry where he was apparently helping her brush her hair, for it was all mussed when I stumbled upon them. And though I would have been a far better choice than he to tend her coif—knowing the intricacies of personal style and hygiene better than most—I held no jealousy whatsoever; for he was simultaneously a braggart and a bore—a seemingly incomprehensible combination that he embodied with ease. He would often bend the ear of any poor soul who happened to be near with tales of his superior and outlandish life. His favorite story being the night he outran the famous Headless Horseman of Sleepy Hollow by crossing St. Amsterdam's Bridge in the nick of time just before he'd been forced into battle with him. Apparently the Horseman, for whatever reason, can't seem to cross St. Amsterdam's Bridge and so Brom claimed victory over the poor, helpless spirit.

But his stories held no interest for me. And his interest in Katrina brought about no jealously whatsoever. You see, it mattered not to me. I wasn't in love with her. What I did feel for her though was sorrow. Brom Bones was a persistent troll who wouldn't take no for an answer. I didn't want to see poor Katrina live out her days with such a beast and an ogre, and so I did what any respectable man *must* do to keep her from doom's door—I made love to the woman.

[*He again smiles grandly.*]

Oh, not in the physical sense (please!), but with words of love, with pampering looks, and by listening to her as if I was really interested. You see, it wasn't for *me* that I was doing it, it was for *her*. To save her from Brom Bones. And I must say, I played the part of the young lover quite well. Everyone was convinced that I had actually fallen for her. And the ruse worked. Daily Brom Bones got more irritable, more depressed, and more desperate. But I refused to let up. I, after all, was saving her. It was a duty; a calling!

[*Quite pleased with himself.*]

I've often fancied myself a hero because of that—sacrificing myself for the good mental health of another. Not a one of you would have done the same, I'm certain. But I've become sidetracked. Ultimately, I know all you gossipmongers want is the climax of the tale when I encountered the Headless Horseman. So, I will prolong your agony no longer.

[*As if telling a mysterious ghost story.*]

It was very late one autumn night. Van Aiken Lane was quiet and still. I could hear the church bells—a good half mile away in the distance—strike twelve o'clock midnight. The air was cold and damp, and I shivered repeatedly as my horse made its way gingerly through the thick fog that clung low to the ground. Although there was a full moon, Van Aiken Lane was black as coal due to the long, outstretched arms of the sycamores, which had not yet lost their leaves, and the long, dangling grape vines that hung precariously low and close to my face. Every so often one would reach out and grab me around the neck!—my escape coming only when I whipped my poor gelding to trot faster than he was able. I was staying with the Dusseldorfs that week, and the closest route home from the Van Tassel residence was down Van Aiken Lane, past the Old Dutch Cemetery, and over St. Amsterdam's Bridge. Now, I'm sure you're asking yourself, "What in Heaven's name was Ichabod Crane doing out alone at such a late and ungodly hour that night?" I'll tell you.

[*With lightness in his voice.*]

Earlier that evening the Van Tassels had thrown a wonderfully lavish party—presumably in my honor, although that bit of information seems to have been accidentally omitted from the invitations. The party provided me with one of the heartiest feasts I ever received in the Hollow. A true smorgasbord: kidney pie, shepherd's pie, apple pie...

[*Realizing he's gotten carried away.*]

Oh, and Miss Van Tassel? Yes, she was there too—by my side the entire time. In fact, the poor thing couldn't keep her hands off me. I suppose that raised an eyebrow or two, and inevitably led to the floury of rumors that ran around the room like a dog after its tail.

I had just gotten through the buffet for the second time when who walks in but that abnormally large Brom Bones. I nearly lost my appetite—a more homely and arrogant fellow I never have seen. His first stop, naturally, was to greet the guest of honor, although I received nothing more than a grunt before his attention turned to Miss Van Tassel. The giant oaf wouldn't be able to utter a proper salutation even if Good Afternoon was his first and last name. At any rate, Miss Van Tassel was clearly annoyed with his presence, for she took my arm, and with that giggle in her voice that she reserved only for me, swept me into the back parlor before I'd even finished filling my plate. I cannot say whether she needed immediate

lovemaking or whether she simply wanted to gaze at me—
many women do, you know—but she clearly was "in the
mood." I, on the other hand, couldn't stop thinking of that
chicken pot pie I had yet to sample. Nevertheless, there we
were—alone—together. The woman was making
protestations of love and all that when suddenly I noticed my
shoe had come untied. So, I merely bent down to retie it—
here, let me demonstrate.

[*He comes around to the side of the podium.*]

I knelt down to retie my shoe and…well, surely you can see
how this could be misconstrued. Then, while I was kneeling
there, who enters but the hippo himself—Brom Bones. Well,
naturally, he thought I was proposing, and Katrina thought I
was proposing, and I was in the midst of tying my shoe when
suddenly Brom knocks me over with a blow to the ribs and
off he goes dragging poor Katrina behind.

Now, it's at this point that I'm sure you expect me to say that
I chased after him. But, you see, I noticed the remains of a
muffin I had pocketed squishing out of my pants. Well,
naturally, I had to dispose of the evidence—it was blueberry
and delicious—and by the time I returned to the party, Brom
had fled with Katrina in hand. All the party was abuzz and
astir. Apparently, it was the scandal (and the highlight) of
their social season. Though others were concerned for my
well-being—looking upon me as the jilted lover—I really
gave it no thought at all. Instead, I kept myself busy at the

buffet—the chicken pot pie was well worth the wait, I'll have you know—where I shared small talk with a variety of incompetents until Katrina returned alone from the garden thirty-two minutes later.

Once again she whisked me off to the back parlor—where I simply *had* to take a few minutes and brush her mussed hair—and there and then she proposed a tête-à-tête alone with me following the party. Hmmm...women just adore me.

[*Spotting a woman in the audience.*]

You do, don't you? You've been staring at me all evening. At any rate, the party broke up and I soon found myself alone with her. Well, the poor thing nearly threw herself at me, begging that I marry her, so as to save her from a miserable life with that stuffed buffalo that had recently dragged her off. I gave it a bit of thought. But I simply couldn't sacrifice my *entire life* for the poor bedraggled waif, and I told her so in no uncertain terms. Well, the poor thing was just crushed—as I'm sure you can imagine—and crumbled into a hundred tiny tears right before my eyes. It really was embarrassing.

But I was adamant. I told her I approved of her friendship but that was all there was to it. I tried to let her down easily—I didn't want to blow my chance of spending another week or two in that lavish house. And that was that. I gathered my hat and coat, and a particularly sweet-looking pumpkin from the buffet table, and headed for home.

So…we return to Van Aiken Lane. As I said, I mounted my nag and in the chill of the night, he and I headed away from the Van Tassel residence and down the dark, winding, tree-lined road. The quiet of the night was interrupted only by the occasional bark of an angry dog…

[*He barks.*]

…or the hoot of a startled owl.

[*He hoots.*]

Suddenly, as my steed and I continued down the lane, I heard from behind me the hooves of another rider. I could hear it getting closer and closer; traveling faster and faster. The horse and rider were moving at a full gallop! He came up upon me. I felt a cold, damp wind brush past my face. Then all of a sudden the rider shouted out to me, "Good evening, Ichabod! Lovely gala, what?" and he raced on right by. It was drunken Mr. Moody making his way home from the party. The man was so intoxicated he turned backwards in his saddle and waved me good-bye as his horse carried him 'til they disappeared down the path.

I soon came upon the Old Dutch Cemetery—and the long line of headstones filled with the names of dead soldiers who'd fought in the Revolution. Van Dyke, Van Buren, Van Rhine. We walked on; grave after grave, plot after plot, body after body. Some graves had flowers, while others only weeds;

still others had been obviously forgotten long ago. I could see each name clearly etched into the stones, for the road had widened, the trees had disappeared, and the full moon now shone brightly, lighting everything in shadows of gray and black. As we made our way toward the church—a short distance from the bridge—a clip-clop sound came a-tapping from behind. Clip-clop, clip-clop, closer, closer, faster, faster. Could it be another drunken reveler, I thought, racing to get past the cemetery grounds. Clip-clop, clip-clop. Faster, faster, closer, closer. The sound began to grow and grow and wild laughter began echoing in the Hollow. I kept my sights in front of me, my eyes glued to the road, when a shadow began to engulf me. The moon was growing dim as the shadow grew and grew until it had overtaken me. A piercing cackle screeched from behind...

[*He cackles.*]

It was loud and long and scared the birds right out of the trees. But not I—no, not I. As I reached the edge of the bridge, I glanced behind me and out of the mist a figure arose—and out of the mist a figure arose—and *there he was*! A horse in full stride and a horseman with no head! A large, strong, impressive presence holding in one arm what appeared to be the horseman's very own head. The horse reared up and whinnied a cry; the horseman cackled and threatened my very existence. But was I scared?! Not on your life!! I rode across the bridge—across which I was told the

Horseman could not pass—got off my horse and stood right up to him! I said, "You go away this instant!" (Timid, my ass!) At which point the Horseman raised his head above his head—or where his head should have been—and there it turned into a bright red ball of fire which he hurled at me with great delight. "Ha-ha-ha!" he screamed as the gruesome appendage shot straight for my head. "Ha-ha-ha!" I said in return. "Ha-ha-*haaa!*"

[*Much calmer.*]

Now, here's where details over the years have gotten a bit sketchy. Some accounts have the ball of fire knocking my own head from my shoulders where it shattered on the ground like a smashed pumpkin; and that my body and soul were "spirited away" by the Horseman and taken to the nether regions, never to be seen again. Well, simply put, I was not "spirited away" that night by the evil Horseman—and I am here tonight as proof of that. Nor was my head turned into a pumpkin and smashed along the roadside. What *was* smashed was the actual pumpkin I had procured from the buffet table for my late night dessert. I merely dropped it while dodging the fireball which had been hurled at me.

[*Back to the story with intense interest.*]

At any rate, after his head had been thrown and extinguished in a puddle, I yelled at the vision with the strength of twenty generals, "Go away, you vile creature, or I'll rip off all your other limbs!" And the Great Headless Horseman rose up from the ground with a cackle and a laugh and a whinny and a fart, and the rider and its stallion evaporated into the mist and were gone—gone!—never to be seen again. You see, it was I—yes, I—who scared away the Horseman and not the other way around! And that, my friends, is what *really* happened when I encountered the Headless Horseman of Sleepy Hollow. The explanation of the Horseman's appearance is usually flippantly dismissed as merely Brom Bones in disguise; the idea being that he intended to scare me away from his dear Miss Van Tassel by playing upon my belief in the supernatural. Oh, what an easy and uneducated conclusion to reach, brought about by men who prefer to hear themselves talk—loudly and at length—rather than chronicle the truth.

[*With disgust.*]

Yes, I'm speaking of writers. A despicable lot—all of them! The truth is the Headless Horseman was a spirit from beyond. It's as simple as that. Some of you, I can tell, are non-believers. But it matters not to me. For I know the truth; you see, I was there and you were not. The Horseman was clearly a restless soul of the Revolution whose head had been blown off by a cannonball, and who had returned to earth seeking vengeance. It's all very clear, don't you see? I, however, not being responsible for the loss of the Horseman's head was never in any danger; and once he recognized that, he vanished into the night like fog in the sun.

As to my disappearance from Sleepy Hollow following this encounter—which is usually described as a frantic fleeing for my life (please!)—there is a very simple and straightforward explanation. My horse, being shaken to the bone by this encounter, raced along furiously and took a wrong turn after crossing the bridge onto Tarry Town Road—the main route out of town. By the time I realized his mistake, I had already crossed the border back into Connecticut; and, well, having already gone that far, figured I might as well return home and visit my family. The next day—having quite a reputation in my hometown—I was offered a teaching position there—one much closer to home. And it is there that I have remained for the past forty-nine years.

So, as you can see, I was an innocent bystander in all of this. I did not bring about Brom's jealousy, or Katrina's unhappy life, and I certainly didn't deserve to be chased down like a common criminal by a horseman with no head. It all remains a mystery to me. But that was many years ago. Last I heard, Miss Van Tassel married that large, bovine-shaped man and they bore seven fat little children—all of whom resembled Brom—even the girls. I can only imagine the width of her hips after seven consecutive childbirths.

[*He shudders with disgust.*]

Many years later I heard through the grapevine that the poor dear was quite happy with her choice of men and the life that had been bestowed upon her. Oh, Katrina. How brave of you to put up such a front for the sake of the children; truly an admirable attempt to keep them from suicide or some other grizzly end. Untimely, though, Katrina Van Tassel made the biggest mistake of her life...

[*A cackle of disgust is heard in the distance. It is so distant it is almost inaudible.* ICHABOD *continues on without taking notice.*]

She chose a man—Brom Bones—who was completely wrong for her...

[*Another cackle, a bit closer.*]

And is now forced to feign love at the expense of her own wants and desires and needs...

[*Still another cackle, even closer.*]

Simply put, Katrina Van Tassel is a stupid woman.

[*With that, the* HEADLESS HORSEMAN *comes riding or flying into the theater and attacks* ICHABOD CRANE, *who runs for his life. The menacing spirit laughs and cackles as he attacks the aged and weak* ICHABOD. *The lights flicker and fade as the* HORSEMAN *moves rapidly about.* ICHABOD *screams with terror and just barely avoids scaring himself to death when the* HORSEMAN *disappears as fast as he came.*]

[*NOTE: It's not important how the effect of the* HORSEMAN *is accomplished: whether through shadows, puppetry, video, or a second actor—it could even be as simple as a lighting and sound effect. What is important, however, is that it be a true moment of fright. It should take the audience by surprise and, without humor, make them sit up in their seats. They must believe that the Headless Horseman exists.*]

There! There! Did you see it? Did you?! The Horseman… The Horseman! The Headless Horseman rides again! Let that be a lesson to you—all of you—especially you who don't believe. The Horseman is real—he exists—he is here. He is always here! Always! You see, I'm *not* insane! I'm *not*! I said he was real, and he is! If I were you, I'd watch my step tonight. Especially while traveling over bridges. For you never know when the Headless Horseman—or any other spirit from beyond—will visit you. But remember: he brings a message— he *always* brings a message. And it's up to you to unmask it, and listen to it, and heed it. Or else be damned.

[*The lights are restored.* ICHABOD *is clearly shaken but attempts to recapture his composure.*]

I must go, and I suggest you do the same. Go! Don't say I didn't warn you.

[ICHABOD *gathers his notes and hurries offstage. There is a subtle, distant cackle of laughter heard from the* HORSEMAN *as the lights fade to black.*]

Murray Schisgal

Queenie

from

The Best American
Short Plays 2002–2003

scene

A park bench on the east side of Central Park.

time

Spring; Saturday, noon

[*At rise:* LAWRENCE ALBERTSON *enters, right, whistling cheerfully, perhaps the waltz from* Der Rosenkavalier.]

[*On a leash following him is* QUEENIE, *a smooth-haired fox terrier or a dog of similar size. Both owner· and animal are groomed to a splendid shine.* LAWRENCE *is sixty-two years of age: he can easily pass for a man ten years younger: He wears a cashmere turtle-neck sweater; an English hacking jacket, gabardine khaki slacks, and cordovan jodhpurs; a pair of knit gloves dangle from his jacket's breast pocket. He passes the bench once, turns about, walks back to sit on bench. He beats the bench with his open hand.*]

LAWRENCE   Up here, Queenie! Up! Up, sweetheart! Up!
Up!

[QUEENIE *jumps up on the bench. In the event that she doesn't
respond to a specific command, the actor is given license to improvise
whatever lines are necessary to accommodate her behavior; always,
however, with shameless affection.*]

That's the girl. That's my good girl. You are the best. The
best there is. Did I ever tell you how much I enjoy walking
with you, huh? Did I? Did I? I can't imagine what I'd do with
myself if you weren't around, my little friend.

[*He muzzles and pats* QUEENIE *on the rump.*]

The irony is that when I first saw you in the pet shop on
Madison Avenue... Do you realize it was almost three years
ago! Three years!

[*Reflectively.*]

Time. Time. Where does it go? Not the most scrupulous and
attentive observation can alter... it's irrevocable momentum.
Pity. Pity.

[*Said quickly.*]

Pity, pity, pity, pity.

[*Comes out of it.*]

Where was I? Oh, yes. Three years ago it was, when I first saw you. I hadn't the slightest intention of taking you home with me. I actually started walking away, heading down the street to Vito's. I did, I did, honest Injun! I don't know what got into me. Maybe it was the way you kept scratching at the window and making those shrill, yelping noises that sounded more like birds chirping than it did a dog barking. I made an abrupt about-face and I walked into the shop and once the sales boy placed you in my arms...I was sold. You were the cutest, cuddliest little creature I had ever seen in my entire life. I admit it. It was love at first sight, right from the start. I took you along with me into Vito's and showed you off to those Saturday afternoon martini drinkers and hangers-on. Afterwards I picked up my ready-to-go lunch of grilled calamari, pasta pomodoro, and broccoli rabe, and I straightaway took you home.

[*He lifts* QUEENIE, *holds her in front of him.*]

Can you imagine the change you made in my life, huh? Can you? Can you? You were the first...living thing who shared my apartment with me in years; literally, literally in years. What a change it was. What a wonderful change. To get up in the morning to the sound of your playful barking, your incessant jumping up and down on the bed, licking at my face, pulling at the covers, not giving me a moment's peace until I'm up and moving to the refrigerator to pour you a bowlful of cold milk.

[*Laughing; scratching at* QUEENIE*'s ear.*]

What a rascal you are. What a devil. Even after I've fed you, you won't let me be until I've showered and dressed sufficiently to take you out for your first walk of the day. And how utterly rejuvenating it is, getting outdoors when the air is still fresh and uncontaminated, the sun just peeking above the horizon... One is glad to be alive... that early in the morning.

[*Scans the sky.*]

One looks up at the luminous, infinite blue sky and prays... without quite knowing why or to whom, feeling quite silly about it and still... one prays, for another day that brings to us... another early morning... with a luminous, infinite blue sky.

[*To* QUEENIE.]

Oh, that is absolutely the best part of the day for me, those early morning walks in the park with, when there's no one about yet, except for an occasional pet lover like myself.

[LAWRENCE *acts out such a meeting. He puts* QUEENIE *back on the bench beside him. He speaks to an imaginary passerby who is walking his leashed, imaginary dog.*]

Good morning! Good morning! Lovely morning, isn't it? That's a handsome Labrador you have there. I've noticed him running...

[*Points to himself.*]

Mine? Queenie? You like her? You're taken with her intelligence? Her...Her lively disposition? Oh, she's an extraordinary companion. Absolutely extraordinary. You can't imagine the fun the two of us have together. We go everywhere. We...

[*Responds to an interruption.*]

Oh, yes, even when I'm out of town on a business trip. No exceptions to the rule. You don't leave your best friend alone in an apartment for any extended period of time. That's a no-brainer. My partners are well aware of my...Let's call them my prejudices.

[*He takes a brush from his pocket and grooms* QUEENIE.]

I know this may sound strange to you, but perhaps you being a pet owner makes it possible for you to understand my feelings. I don't draw any distinctions whatsoever between a domestic pet and a human being. I am incapable of drawing such a distinction. I find it profoundly abhorrent to...

[*Responds to an interruption.*]

You'll get no argument from me there. The innumerable stories one hears and reads about: the sacrifices made by these domestic pets during fires, burglaries, physical assaults; the accounts of their unselfish devotion and bravery...There's a veritable library filled with such incidents. How any human being can think of being superior in any way whatso...

[*Responds to an interruption.*]

Vivisection? Did you say vivisection? Please, I implore you, don't get me started on that! The very word sends chills down my spine. If there's anything more heinous and unconscionable...

[*Responds to interruption.*]

I agree. Un-for-giv-able. Un-for-giv-able. We best move on to another...

[*Glances at wristwatch.*]

It is getting late. And I must be off. I have to pick up...Why, that is amazing. It is my birthday today. How in the world did you...?

[*Smiles broadly.*]

I guess with the Internet there's no having a private life nowadays. Thank you. Thank you. I appreciate the offer of a toast this evening, but I do have other plans. I'm sure I'll see you around again. Have a good day. Bye now. Bye . . .

[*He waves as the imaginary passerby moves off with his leashed dog. His hand falls to his lap. He continues grooming* QUEENIE; *solemnly.*]

Sixty-two, Queenie. Sixty-two. Gives one . . . food for thought. Pause for reflection. The paramount concern is: Do I retire this year or wait until the big Six Five. I have to admit, I don't enjoy going into the office as much as I used to. The practice of law is no longer of any particular interest to me. All the old fellows are gone and all the new ones strike me as a greedy, uncivilized bunch. Not a gentleman among them. Not a one. Besides, think of all the time we'd have together if I retired. Wouldn't that be fun? Wouldn't you like that? Wouldn't . . .

[*A sigh.*]

I can't believe it. Sixty-two. Sixty-two. Time. Time. Days. Weeks. Months. Years. Did I ever tell you I was once married? Did you know that, Queenie? I must have spoken to you about it.

[*A thoughtful beat.*]

In any event, at the obscenely youthful age of twenty-four, soon after passing the bar exams, on my first try, you should know, I met a woman a year younger than myself through a client of mine.

[*As if searching for the correct pronunciation.*]

Emma. Miss . . . Emma . . . Reynolds.

[*A beat.*]

She was a social worker with the city, very much involved in child abuse cases. We dated, we...fell in love, we married, and we moved into an apartment, a brownstone in Chelsea. We lived as fully and happily as any two young people possibly could.

[*As if searching for the correct pronunciation.*]

Emma. Miss Emma Reynolds. Mrs. Emma...Reynolds...Albertson.

[*He removes a small plastic bag filled with dog biscuits from pocket; he feeds* QUEENIE.]

I tell you, my little friend, our lives could not have proceeded more satisfactorily. I entered the field of entertainment law and immediately found it both lucrative and challenging. Emma moved inexorably up the civil service ladder until she arrived at an administrative position of power and trust. And, I must say, for the five years of our marriage, there wasn't a day that passed that didn't have some special pleasure in store for us, whether it be a particularly outstanding dinner at a newly discovered bistro or, for no apparent reason and due to no deliberate design, an all-night entwining of blissful lovemaking.

[*A sigh.*]

Emma. My wife. My long-lost wife. Memories of what was; what could have been; what is not. She's remarried. With

grown children now. Living…I know not where. Is she
happy? I would think she is. The thrust of her being…
always…Family. Values. Community.

[*A beat.*]

Emma. Miss Emma Reynolds. Mrs. Emma…Reynolds…
Donleavy.

[*A desperate note.*]

You have to understand, Queenie, men and women,
particularly, specifically, young men and young
women…They are not the same. They do not desire the
same things. They do not have the same goals and ambitions.

You can argue, with some justification, that as they grow
older, there is a coming together between the sexes, a joining
of intentions and purposes and, ironically, even a physical
sameness, as they are as babies, when they first come into this
world. But not when they mature. Not when they are in the
first full flush of their…sexual selves; the first full flush of their
visceral, biological selves. Then they are decidedly different.
Decidedly opposites. At odds. At loggerheads. There is no
question about it. Absolutely no question about it.

[*Less emotionally.*]

Simply put, I was not in control of my own life. I was, in fact,
under the control of…under the domination and beck and

call of...an unrelenting sexuality. I was no more than an idiotic, weak-kneed, spineless puppet that was wagged heedlessly about on the strings of a mad puppeteer. That is the simple truth of it.

[*Meditatively.*]

Indeed it was. Indeed it was.

[*A beat.*]

Make no mistake about it, my dear friend, I had no control over my own life from my first year in high school until... until I woke up one morning in the recent past and suddenly realized that I had not fantasized an all-night entwining with some phantasmagoric lady love...in possibly weeks. It was at that particular point of time that I seemingly turned the corner from idiocy to sexual passivity and, once again, took control over my own life after a fifty-year hiatus.

[*A beat; aggressively.*]

As I said before, young men and young women are not the same, contrary to feminist propaganda. If a young woman confessed to being dominated by her libido as ruthlessly as I was, she would be deemed aberrant, afflicted with a pathological condition akin to nymphomania. But the reaction to such a confession from a young man would inevitably evoke a smile, a pat on the back and the gratuitous advice that he take a brisk cold shower.

[*A beat.*]

And so it was with me. So it was, unrelentingly, incessantly.
Even...Even when I was married to Emma.

Miss Emma Reynolds. Mrs. Emma...Reynolds...Donleavy.

[*A beat.*]

Even then, Queenie, even in the throes of my marital bliss,
when I wanted for nothing, desired for nothing, loved dearly
the woman I was living with...Even then my eye roved to
catch a glimpse of an exposed thigh, a well-endowed breast, a
pair of gracefully insinuating buttocks, as my mind conjured
sugar-plum scenarios of an all-night entwining with...
another...another of unfamiliar scent, of unexplored texture,
of unsuspected mysteries. Even then. Even then.

[*He takes a red ribbon from his pocket and makes a bow from it.*]

Still, no matter how helplessly I was lost in my adulterous
fantasies, I observed, faithfully, the vows I had taken.

Perhaps, if Emma had not introduced the thought of our
moving to the suburbs, of our starting a family, buying a
home, perhaps then, I would have observed the vows of our
marriage for the remainder of my days. But once she had
verbalized her deepest desires, her grand design for our
common...future, I...I couldn't...I couldn't relinquish my
fantasies, nor free myself of this...

[*Stares down at his lap.*]

distended abomination sulking between my legs.

[*He finishes knotting the red ribbon and ties it around* QUEENIE'*s neck.*]

Not then. Not at that time. Not at such a...youthful age.

[*A beat.*]

I walked away, Queenie. Of my own volition, I left her. Over thirty years ago. I haven't seen her since. But I've heard from others about her health...her interests...her grown children, three of them, I'm told, and of an amiable husband...who paints on weekends.

[*With vigor:*]

But don't you think for a second that I didn't fulfill every one of those...of those fantasies of mine. Don't you think for a second I didn't have a...a plethora of wildly gratifying and, yes, ecstatic times for myself. Let me tell you, my little friend, I wasn't in the entertainment business for nothing. The possibilities offered to me were limitless. I had, over the years, more lovers of every conceivable size, shape, age, color, temperament, and predilection than you can possibly imagine in a...in a lifetime of Sundays!

[*Slaps his thigh.*]

Damn! I slept with tons of them! Lived with tons of them! Weeks. Months. Trips to Europe, the Far East, Africa, Alaska...You name it and, word of honor, I did it! I had it! I left no bit of pulchritude untouched. No opportunity lost. No invitation ignored. No request denied!

[*Reflectively.*]

In the past, that is. In days gone, that is. Ages ago, it seems.

When I was wagged heedlessly about on the strings of a mad puppeteer.

[*A sigh.*]

Yesterday's meal does not today's stomach fill. Every morning one is hungry. Always hungry. Again. For something. For anything.

[*He picks up* QUEENIE; *hugs her:*]

I'll tell you something, my little friend. It is my candid opinion that I am presently in a position, emotionally in a frame of mind, to entertain the prospect of a permanent union.

[*Impatiently.*]

To put it simply, I'm quite ready to give marriage another go-around. In fact, I've made a concerted effort recently to meet eligible women of…mature years. I must say, I've had enough of these young fly-by-nights. Frankly, they're too insistent on their own pleasures for the likes of me. I just don't have the patience for them anymore. I did start dating, making inquiries, overtures. In good faith. Without condition or prejudice. And yet…Maybe it's just a spell of bad luck I've been having. So far I haven't been able to connect, to find someone who is compatible, someone with whom I can be…comfortable, like I was with Emma…Miss Emma Reynolds. Mrs. Emma…Reynolds…Donleavy.

[*Ruefully.*]

I guess there's no second-guessing who we meet, when we meet, how we meet. Statistically, the odds are heavily against us ever finding someone with whom we're comfortable with.

[*He's lost in reverie for a beat before shaking himself to movement.*]

But enough of this! Let's be off!

[*He rises, leash in hand, as* QUEENIE *jumps off the bench. With his free hand, he brushes off his slacks.*]

We'll pick up our lunch at Vito's: grilled calamari, pasta pomodoro, and broccoli rabe for me; a nice osso bucco meat bone for you. And, oh, yes, if I forget you must remind me: a chilled bottle of sauvignon blanc.

[*He moves off, left.*]

After all, today is my birthday. We have to celebrate the occasion. In style.

[*Pulling on leash.*]

Come along, Queenie. Come along, sweetheart.

[*And they exit, with* LAWRENCE *singing to himself, "Happy birthday to me…Happy birthday to me…," using the name "Larry" in the appropriate line, as he exits stage with* QUEENIE.]

Shel Silverstein

The Devil and Billy Markham

from

The Best American
Short Plays 1991–1992

[*The* STORYTELLER *enters. He wears a ratty topcoat, baggy pants, unmatching vest, wrinkled shirt, and spotted necktie. He carries a mop and a bucket. He sets down the bucket and begins to mop the floor, humming to himself. He looks up, surprised to see the audience. He realizes his opportunity. He smiles. He begins to recite.*]

The Devil walked into Linebaugh's on a rainy Nashville
　　night.
While the lost souls sat and sipped their soup in the sickly
　　yellow neon light.
And the Devil he looked around the room, and he got down
　　on one knee.
He says, "Is there one among you scum who'll roll the dice
　　with me?"
Red, he just strums his guitar, pretending not to hear.

And Eddie, he just looks away and takes another sip of beer.
Vince, he says, "Not me, I'll pass. I've had my share of Hell."
And kept scribbling on a napkin some song he was sure would
    sell.
Ronnie just kept whisperin' low to the snuff queen who
    clutched at his sleeve.
And somebody coughed—and the Devil scoffed
And turned on his heel to leave.
"Hold on," says a voice from the back of the room,
"'Fore you walk out that door.
If you're looking for some action, friend, well, I've rolled some
    dice before."
And there stood Billy Markham, he'd been on the scene for
    years,
Singing all those raunchy songs that the town didn't want to
    hear.
He'd been cut and bled a thousand times, and his eyes were
    wise and sad.
And all his songs were songs of the street, and all of his luck
    was bad.
"I know you," says Billy Markham, "from many a dark and
    funky place,
But you always spoke in a different voice and wore a different
    face.
While me, I've gambled here on Music Row with hustlers,
    hacks, and whores
And my dues are paid. I ain't afraid to roll them dice of yours."

"Well then, get down," says the Devil, "and put that guitar
    away,
And take these dice in your luckless hands and I'll tell you
    how this game is played.
You get one roll—and you bet your soul—and if you roll
    thirteen you win.
And all the joys of flesh and gold are yours to touch and
    spend.
But if that thirteen don't come up, then kiss your ass good-bye,
And will your useless bones to God, 'cause your goddamn
    soul is mine."
"Thirteen?" says Billy Markham. "Hell, I've played in
    tougher games.
I've loved ambitious women and I've rode on wheelless trains.
So gimme room, you stinkin' fiend, and let it all unwind,
Nobody's rolled a thirteen yet, but this just might be the time."
Then Billy Markham, he takes the dice, and the dice feel
    heavy as stones.
"They should," the Devil says, " 'cause they're carved outa
    Jesus' bones!"
And Billy Markham turns the dice and the dice they have no
    spots.
"I'm sorry," says the Devil, "but they're the only ones I got."
"Well, shit," says Billy Markham. "Now I really don't mean to
    bitch,
But I never thought I'd stake my roll in a sucker's game like
    this."

"Well then, walk off," says the Devil. "Nobody's tied you
      down."
"Walk off where?" says Billy. "It's the only game in town.
But I just wanna say 'fore I make my play, that if I should
      chance to lose,
I will this guitar to some would-be star who'll play some
      honest blues.
Who ain't afraid to sing the words like damn or shit or fuck,
And who ain't afraid to put his ass on the stage where he
      makes his bucks.
But if he plays this guitar safe, and sings some sugary lies,
I'll haunt him till we meet in Hell—now gimme them fuckin'
      dice."
And Billy Markham shakes the dice and yells, "C'mon . . .
      thirteen."
And the dice they roll—and they come up—blank.
"You lose!" the Devil screams.
"But I really must say 'fore we go our way that I really do like
      your style.
Of all the fools I've played and beat, you're the first one who
      lost with a smile."
"Well, I'll tell you somethin'," Billy Markham says.
"Those odds weren't too damn bad. In fourteen years on
      Music Row, that's the best damn chance I've had."
Then the Devil takes Billy under his cloak, and they walk out
      through Linebaugh's door,
Leavin' Billy's old guitar there on the sawdust floor.

And if you go to Linebaugh's now, you can see it there today.
Hangin'…from a nail on that wall of peelin' gray…
Billy Markham's old guitar…
That nobody dares to play.

BILLY MARKHAM AND THE FLY

Billy Markham slowly turns on a white hot spit,
And his skin it crackles like a roasting pig, and his flesh is
     seared and split,
And sulphur fills his nostrils and he's fed on slime and mud,
By a hairy imp with a pointed stick who bastes him in spider's
     blood,
And his eyeballs boil up inside his skull and his throat's too
     charred to scream.
So he sleeps the sleep of the burning dead and he dreams
     unspeakable dreams.
Then in walks the Devil, puttin' little screaming skulls as the
     bells of Hell start clangin',
And his last shot rolls right up to Billy Markham's toes
And he says, "Hey, Bill, how're they hanging'?
I'm sorry we couldn't give you a tomb with a view, but right
     now this is the best we got.
But as soon as we're done with Attila the Hun, we'll move
     you right into his spot.

Have you met your neighbors? Have you heard them scream?
    Do they keep you awake in the fire?
Hey, a little more brimstone on number nine—and hoist up
    them thumbs a bit higher.
Ah, you can't get good help these days, Bill, and there ain't
    much profit in Hell.
No, turn that adulteress upside down—do I have to do
    everything myself?
I tell you, Bill, it's a full-time job, tending these red hot coals,
And all this shovelin' and stokin', fryin' and smokin', proddin'
    and pokin', stretchin' and chokin', why I hardly got time
    for collecting new souls.
Which brings me to the subject of my little visit, now you're
    one of them natural-born gamblin' men,
And I'll bet you'd give most anything to get those dice in your
    hands again.
So instead of swimming in this muck and slime and burning
    crisp as [*Tastes him.*] toast…
I'll trade you one roll…of the dice for the souls…of the ones
    who love you most."
"Trade the souls of the ones who love me most? Not a chance
    in Hell I will."
"Spoken like a hero," the Devil says. "Hey, a little more fire
    for Bill."
"You can roast me, bake me, or boil me," says Billy.
"Go and have your fiendish fun.
A coward dies a thousand times—a brave man dies but once."

"Oh, beautiful, sensitive, and poetic too," says the Devil.

"But life ain't like no rhyme.

And I know ways to make a brave man die a million times."

"Hey, take your shot...Throw what you got...But I won't
    trade love away."

"That's what they all say," laughs the Devil, ". . . but when I
    turn up the fire, they play."

And the flame burns white and Bill's flesh burns black and he
    smells his roasting stink.

And the hell rats nibble upon his nose...and Billy begins to
    think.

He thinks about his sweetheart who loved him through his
    crazy days.

He thinks of his gray-haired momma, hell, she's gettin' old
    anyway.

He thinks of his baby daughter—he ain't seen her since last fall.

He thinks about walkin' the earth again and he thinks of the
    horrible pain he's in, and he thinks of the game that he
    just might win and he yells, "Hey—take 'em all."

And—*zap*—He's back again at Linebaugh's, kneeling on that
    same old floor.

And across from him the Devil squats, ready to play once more.

"I guess my point is still thirteen?" Billy Markham asks.

"The point's the same," the Devil sneers. "But the stakes are
    your loved ones' asses."

"Well, one never knows," Billy Markham says, "when lady
    luck's gonna smile on a man.

And if a charcoal corpse from Hell can't roll thirteen, then
    who the hell can?"
And Billy Markham shakes the dice and whispers, "Please,
    thirteen."
And the dice roll out a...six...and a...six...and then, as if in
    a dream...
A buzzing fly from a plate nearby, like a messenger sent from
    heaven,
Shits—right in the middle of one of them sixes—and turns it
    into a seven.
"Thirteen! Thirteen! Thirteen! Thirteen! I have beat the
    Devil's play."
"Oh, have you now," the Devil says, and—*whoosh*—he blows
    that speck away.
"Which only proves," the Devil says, "that Hell's too big to buck,
And when you're gambling for your ass, don't count on fly-shit
    luck."
"Well, luck and love..." sighs Billy Markham, "they never do
    last for long,
But y'know that fly shittin' on that die would have made one
    hell of a song."
"You're a songwriting fool," the Devil grins. "There ain't no
    doubt about it.
As soon as you go and lose one damn game, you wanna write
    a song about it.
But there's a whole lot more to life and death than the rhymes
    and tunes you give 'em.

And any fool can sing the blues, [*Sings.*] any fool can sing the
    blues, any fool can sing the blues, let's see if you can live
    'em."

Then—*zap!*—Billy wakes up back in Hell, bein' stuffed with
    white hot coals.

While imps dance on his head and shit in his hair and wipe
    their asses with his soul . . .

And he hears the screams of his momma as she turns in the
    purple flame.

And he hears the cries of his baby girl as she pays the price of
    his game.

He hears the voice of his own true love laugh like a child at play,

As she satisfies the Devil in her own sweet lovin' way.

And buzzin' 'cross Bill's bumin' bones and landing on his
    starin' eye,

And nibblin' on his roastin' flesh is the grinnin' Linebaugh's fly.

BILLY MARKHAM'S
LAST ROLL

"Good morning, Billy Markham, it's time to rise and shine."

The Devil's word come grindin' into Billy's bumin' mind.

And he opens up one bloodshot eye to that world of living
    death.

And he feels the Devil's bony claw and he smells his rotten
    breath.

"Wake up, Sunshine!" the Devil laughs. "I'm giving you
    another turn."

"I'm turning now," Billy Markham growls. "Go away and let
    me burn."

"Well, you sure are a grouch when you wake up, but you
    wouldn't let a chance go by."

"Another chance to roll thirteen? Hey, stick it where your fire
    don't shine.

I've played your game, now I feel the shame, as I hear my
    loved ones' cries,

And I'll piss on your shoe, if ever you come near me again
    with them fly-shit dice."

"Dice? Dice? Who said dice? Anybody hear me say dice?

Hey, imp, pour my buddy here a cool glass of water and
    throw in a nice big chunk of ice."

"And since when," says Billy, "do you go around handing out
    gifts,

Except pokes from your burning pitchfork or buckets full of
    boiling shit?"

"Well, it's Christmas," says the Devil, "and all of us down
    here below,

We sort of celebrate in our own special way, and this year
    you're the star of the show.

Why, just last night I was up on Earth and I seen that lovers'
    moon,

And I said to myself, 'Hey, I bet ol' Billy could use a little poon.'"

"Poon?" says Billy Markham. "Last thing I need is poon.

Talk about gettin' my ashes hauled, hell, I'll be all ashes soon."

"Damn! Damn! Damn!" cries the Devil. "He's been too long
on the fire.

I told you imps to fry him slow, now you gone and burned out
his desire.

You gotta leave 'em some hope, leave 'em some dreams, so
they know what Hell is for,

'Cause when a man forgets how sweet love is, well, Hell ain't
Hell no more.

So just to refresh your memory, Billy, we're gonna send you
back to Earth.

And I'll throw in a little Christmas blessing to remind you
what life is worth.

For exactly thirteen hours, you can screw who you want to
screw,

And there ain't no creature on God's green earth who is
gonna say no to you.

While me and all these burning souls and all my imps and
fiends,

We're gonna sit down here and watch you on that big twenty-
four-inch color screen.

And we'll see each hump you're humpin', and we'll hear each
grunt you groan,

And we'll laugh like hell at the look upon your face when it's
time to come back home."

"Well, a chance is a chance is a chance," says Billy, steppin'
down off the sizzlin' coals.

"But what if one won't gimme none, what if one says 'no'?"
"No? What if one says 'no'? Ain't nobody gonna say 'no.'
Nobody quits or calls in sick when the Devil calls the show.
Not man nor woman nor beast!" shouts the Devil. "And no
    'laters' or 'maybes' or 'buts,'
And before one soul says 'no' to you I will see these Hell
    gates rust.
But...if anyone refuses you, I say, anyone you name,
Then you'll be free to stay on Earth, now get out and play the
    game!"
Then a flash of light...and a thunderclap...and Billy's back
    on Earth once more,
And the asphalt sings beneath his feet as he swings toward
    Music Row.
First he stops in at the Exit Inn to seduce the blond on the
    door,
Then the RCA receptionist he takes on the office floor.
He nails the waitress down at Mack's, the one with the
    pear-shaped breasts, and four of the girls from BMI
    right on Frances Preston's desk.
He screws his way from MCA to Vanderbilt's ivy walls,
And he pokes everything that giggles or sings or whimpers or
    wiggles or crawls.
First Debbie, then Polly, then Dotty, then Dolly, then
    Jeannie, and Jessie and Jan,
Then Marshall and Sal and that redheaded gal who takes the
    tickets down at Opryland.

And Brenda and Sammy and Sharon and Sandy, Loretta and
Buffy and May,
And Terri and Lynne at the Holiday Inn and Joey and Zoe
and Faye.
Then Sherry and Rita and Diane and Anita, Olivia, Emmy
and Jean,
And Donna and Kay down at Elliston Place—right there in
the pinto beans.
Then Hazel and Carla and an ex-wife of Harlan's, then Melva
and Marge and Marie,
And three fat gospel singers who all come together in perfect
three-part harmony.
He is humpin' the Queen of Country Music, when he hears
the Devil moan.
"Make it sweet, Billy Markham, but make it short, you've got
just thirty seconds to go.
And all of us here, we're applauding your show, and we'd say
you done right well,
And we just can't wait to hear you moan, when you're fuckless
forever in Hell."
"Hold on!" says Billy, with one last thrust. "If I got thirty
seconds mo',
Then I got the right to one last hump before it's time to go."
"Well, raise your voice and make your choice but you'd better
be quick and strong,
And make it a cum to remember, Bill—it's gotta last you
eternity long.

So who will it, who will it, who will it be? Who's gonna be the
    one?
Starlet or harlot or housewife or hippie or grandma or
    schoolgirl or black-robed nun?
Or fresh-scented virgin or dope-smokin' groupie or sweet
    ever-smilin' Stew?"
And Billy Markham, he stops…and he looks at them all and
    he says to the Devil…"I think I'll…take *you*!"
"Foul!" cries the Devil. "Foul, no fair! The rules don't hold
    for me."
"You said man or woman or beast," says Billy, "and I guess
    you're all of the three."
And a roar goes up from the demons of Hell and it shakes the
    earth across,
And the imps all squeal and the fiends they scream,
"He's gonna fuck the Boss!"
"Why you filthy scum," the Devil snarls to Billy, blushing a
    fiery red.
"I give you a chance to live again and you bust me in front of
    my friends."
"Hey, play or pay," Billy Markham says, "so set me free at
    last,
Or raise your tail and hear all Hell wail when I bugger your
    devilish ass."
"OK, OK, OK, you win. Go on back to your precious Earth.
And plod along and plug your songs, but carry this lifelong
    curse.

You shall lust for a million women and not one's gonna come
    your way,
And you shall write ten million songs and not one's ever
    gonna get played.
And your momma and daughter and your own true love they
    gonna stay down here with me,
And you'll carry the guilt like a movable Hell wherever the
    hell you be."
So back on the streets goes Billy again, eatin' them
    Linebaugh's beans,
Singin' his songs while nobody listens and tellin' his story
    that no one believes
And gets no women and he gets no hits but he says just what
    he thinks,
Hey, buy him a round...it won't cost much...ice water's all
    he drinks.
But try not to stare at the burns on his wrists as he wipes the
    sweat from his head,
As he tells how the Devil burned him black
But he turned the Devil red.

BILLY, SCUZZY, AND GOD

We're at the Purple Peacock Rhinestone Bar, all the low are
    getting high,
And Billy tells his tale again to anyone who'll buy.

With waving arms and rolling eyes, he screams to the
        drunken throng,
"I've whipped the Devil and lived through Hell, now who's
        gonna sing my songs?"
Then from the shadows comes an oily voice. "Hey, kid, I like
        your moves."
And out of the back limps a little wizened cat,
With black-and-white perforated wing-tipped shoes.
"Sleezo's the name," the little man says, "but I'm Scuzzy to
        my friends.
And I think I got a little business proposition you just might
        be interested in."
"Scuzzy Sleezo hisself," Billy Markham says. "Man, you're a
        legend in these woods,
You never cut the Devil down, but you done damn near as good.
Why, since I been old enough to jack, I been hearin' your
        greasy name.
It's an honor to meet an all-star scuzz. Where you setting up
        your game?"
"No more games for me," says Scuzzy. "I'm too old and too
        slow for the pace.
So I'm the world's greatest hustler's *agent* now and, Billy, I
        been studying your case.
I seen your first match with the Devil, and son, it was a
        Volkswagen–Mack truck collision.
And your second shot, well, you showed me a lot, but you got
        burned in a hometown decision.

And I says to myself, 'He can go all the way, with the proper
   guidance of course.
The kid's got the heart, and with a few more smarts, he'd be
   an irresistible force.'
Yeah, I can show you the tricks and show you the shticks just
   like a hustler's training camp.
And I'll bring you on slow—then a prelim or so—then—
   powee!—a shot at the Champ."
"The Champ?" says Billy Markham. "Now who in God's
   name is that?"
"Why God himself," says Scuzzy, "you know anybody more
   champ than that?"
"Hey, a match with God?" Billy Markham grins.
"And what would be the purse?"
"Why, a seat in Heaven forever, of course, 'stead of livin' this
   no pussy, no hits, no nuthin' Nashville curse.
But I'll drive you like a wagon, son, and I'll sweat you like a
   Turk.
All for just 50 percent of the take—now sign here and let's get
   to work."

Now we find ourselves at the funky pool hall known as the
   Crystal Cue,
And the time is three months later, and the smoke is thick and
   blue.
And the pool table cloth is stained with tears and blood and
   ketchup spots.

As a fat old man with a dirty white beard stands practicin'
     three cushion shots.
"What are we doin' here?" says Billy to Scuzzy. "I been
     taught and I been trained.
And I don't need no more prelims, I am primed for the Big
     Big Game."
"Well, son," says the old man, sinkin' the four, "why don't
     you pick yourself out a cue?"
"Hey, Santa Claus," Billy Markham snaps back, "wasn't
     nobody talkin' to you.
"Whoa, whoa," Scuzzy says, pullin' Billy aside..."if you look
     close, you will notice his cue is a lightning rod.
And he ain't no Santa, and he ain't Fat Daddy...you just
     insulted God."
"Well, hey, excuse me, Lord," says Bill. "I didn't mean to be
     uncool,
But it sure can shake a fellah's faith to find God hustling pool."
"Well, where you expect to find me," says God, "on a throne
     with cherubs around?
Hey, I do that six days and nights a week, but on the seventh
     day...I get down.
Besides I can't believe you came in here just to bat the breeze
     around."
"You're right about that, Lord," Billy says. "I come to take
     your crown."
"Beg pardon, Lord," says Scuzzy Sleezo. "I don't mean no
     disrespect.

But when you're dealing with my boy, don't speak to him
      direct.

I'm his agent and representative and this kid is hotter than
      hot,

In his last match, he whipped the Devil, and now we're
      lookin' for a title shot."

"Beat the Devil, you say?" laughs God. "Well, I take my hat
      off to him.

Let him hang up his mouth and pick out a cue and he'll get
      the shot that's due him.

Any game he names—any table he's able—

Any price he can afford."

"Straight pool for heaven," says Billy Markham.

"Straight pool it is," says the Lord.

Crack—Billy Markham wins the break and bust 'em cool and
      clean.

The five ball falls, he sinks the seven, and then devastates the
      thirteen.

He makes the nine, and he bags the eleven, and he puts the
      six away,

Then the three and the eight on a triple combination and he
      wins the game on a smooth masse.

He wins the next game, the next, and the next, and when he
      finally does miss,

He blows the dust off his hands, and his game score stands at
      1376.

"Well, my turn at last," says the Lord chalkin' up.

"Son, you sure shoot a wicked stick.
I'll need some luck to beat a run like that: that is without
       resorting to miracles or tricks."
"Hey, trick and be damned," Billy Markham laughs.
"Tonight I'm as hot as flame.
So I laugh at your tricks—and I sneer at your stick
And I take your name in vain."
"Oooh," goes the crowd that's been gathering around.
"Oooh," goes the rack boy in wonder.
"Oooh," says Scuzzy Sleezo. "I think you just made a slight
       tactical blunder."
"Oooh," says God, "you shouldn't have said that, son, you
       shouldn't have said that at all!"
And his cue cracks out like a thunderbolt spittin' a flamin'
       ball.
It sinks everything on the table, then it zooms up off the
       green.
Through the dirty window with a crash of glass and into the
       wind like a woman's scream.
Out of the pool hall, up through the skies,
The cue ball flames and swirls,
Bustin' in and out of every pool game in the world.
It strikes on every table, it crashes every rack.
And every pool ball in creation comes rebounding back!
Back through the window, they tumble and crash,
Down through the ceiling they spin.
A million balls rain down on the table, and everyone goes in.

"Now, there," says Scuzzy Sleezo, "is a shot you don't see
    every day.

Lord, you should have an agent to handle your press, and
    build up the class of your play.

My partnership with this dirtbag here has come to a
    termination.

But God and Scuzzy Sleezo? Hey, that would be a combination."

Meanwhile, the cue ball flyin' back last, like a sputterin'
    fizzlin' rocket.

Goes weaving dizzily down the table

And—*plunk!*—falls right in the pocket.

"Scratch, you lose," says Billy. "I thought you said you could
    shoot!"

"Scratch," says Scuzzy Sleezo. "I told you my boy'd come
    through."

"Scratch!" murmurs the crowd of hangers and hustlers.

"At last we have seen it all."

"Scratch!" mutters the Lord. "I guess I put a little too much
    English on the ball.

Just another imperfection, I never get it quite on the button.

Tell you what, son, I'll spot you three million balls and play
    you one more double or nothin'."

"Double what?" says Billy Markham. "I already whipped you
    like a child.

And I won my seat in Heaven, now I'm gonna set it awhile."

"Hit-and-run chickenshit," sneers God. "You said you was the
    best.

Turns out you're just a get-lucky-play-it-safe pussy like all the
rest."
"Whoa-whoa," says Billy. "There's somethin' in that voice I
know quite well."
And he reaches out and yanks off God's white beard—and
there stands the Devil himself!
"You said you was God," Billy Markham cries. "You conned
me and hustled me, too!"
"I am God—sometimes—and sometimes I'm the Devil, good
and bad, just like you.
I'm everything and everyone in perfect combination.
And everyone but you knows that there ain't no separation.
[*Sings.*] I'm everything and everyone in perfect combination.
And everyone but you knows . . ."
"Please, please," says Billy Markham. "You ain't that great a
singer.
And I would like to get to Heaven before they stop serving
dinner."
"OK," says God, scribblin' somethin' down. "Give this note
to the angel on the wall.
And you sit up there and plunk your harp . . ."
"Hey, anybody wanna shoot some eight ball?"
So Billy walks out into the parkin' lot with stardust in his eyes,

[*Sings.*]

"I got a seat in Heaven."
And he sees a golden staircase stretchin' up to paradise.

[*Sings.*]

"I got a seat in Heaven."
And he grips the glittering balustrade, and he begins his
    grand ascent.

[*Sings.*]

"I got a…"
"Just a minute, good buddy," yells Scuzzy Sleezo. "How about
    my 50 percent?
I helped you win the championship—and you wouldn't do ole
    Scuzzy Wuzzy wrong,
And since the purse is a seat in Heaven, why, you just gotta
    take me along."
"Just a minute," says Billy Markham. "There's something
    weird going on in this game.
All the voices that I'm hearin' start to sound just the same."
And he rips off Scuzzy Sleezo's face and the Devil's standing
    there.
"Good God," yells Billy Markham, "are you—are you
    everywhere?"
"Yes, I am," the Devil says. "And don't look so damn
    surprised.
I thought you could smuggle me into Heaven wearing my
    Sleezy disguise.
'Course I could've walked in as Jehovah, but it just wouldn't
    have been the same.

But you and your corny Dick Tracy bit—you had to go and
    ruin my fantasy game.
Go on, climb your golden staircase, enjoy your paradise.
But don't rip off your own face, Bill—or you might get a
    shockin' surprise.
But I'll be damned if I let you get to Heaven climbin' that
    golden stairway."
And he plucks out Billy Markham's soul and tees it up, and—
    whack—drives it up the fairway.
And Billy floats out on a sea of light—on a snow white cloud
    he sails,
While vestal virgins comb his hair, and cherubs manicure his nails.
And up, up to glory, Billy Markham sails away,
And high, high above him,
He hears his own songs being played.
While down, down below hear Scuzzy Sleezo curse his name,
To the click-click-click of the pool balls
As God hustles another game.

BILLY MARKHAM'S DESCENT

Billy Markham sits on an unwashed cloud, his hair is matted
    and mussed.
His dusty wings hang limp and grey and his harp strings have
    gone to rust.

With tremblin' hands and tearstained cheeks, and a glazed
    look in his eyes,
He chews his nails and grinds his teeth, and stares across the
    skies.
But his thoughts are down in that nether world, in that
    burning fiery rain.
His thoughts are with his momma, how he longs to soothe
    her pain.
His thoughts are with his baby girl, how he'd love to ease her
    cryin'.
His thoughts are with his own true love, how he'd love to
    bust her spine.
So late that night, while the heavenly harps play "In the
    Sweet Bye and Bye,"
Billy reaches for the silken rope that hangs down from the sky.
He has stripped himself of his crown and robes.
He has clutched the silken cord:
As he swings himself down without a sound, so's not to wake
    the Lord.
Down he winds through the perfumed air, down through the
    marshmallow clouds.
And he hangs for a while o'er the city roofs,
Lookin' down at the scurryin' crowds.
Then down, down, through a manhole, to a stench he knows
    quite well.
Through the sewers of the street, till he feels his feet touch
    the shit-mucked shores of Hell.

Then he scales the crusted rusted gates, and he throws a bone
    to Cerberus hounds.
And he swims the putrid river Styx, still down and farther
    down.
Down past the gluttons, the dealers and pimps, down past the
    murderers' cage.
Down past the rock stars searching in vain for their names on
    the *Rolling Stone* page.
Down past the door of The Merchants of War, past the
    puritans slop-filled bin
Past the bigots' hive, till at last he arrives, at the pit marked
    BLAMELESS SINS.
And he finds the vat where his momma boils: and he raises
    her gently from the deep.
And he finds the grate where his little girl bums: and he lifts
    her and soothes her and rocks her to sleep.
And he finds the pit where his sweetheart sleeps: and he spits
    on the fire where she lay.
And he curses her as a whore of Hell:
Curses and turns away.
"From this day on, I place my faith only in mother and child.
And never again shall I seek sweet salvation
In some bitch's scum stained smile."
Then back through the river he swims with them,
Back over the gate he climbs,
And over the white hot coals he leaps, with the Hellhounds
    barking close behind.

Then back up the silken rope he climbs, up through the
    suffering swarms.
Past the clutching hands and the pitiful screams with his two
    precious loves in his arms.
Just one more pull, just one more pull—then free forever
    from Hell.
Just one more pull then—"Hello, Billy!"—and there stands
    the Devil himself.
And now he's wearing his crimson robes and his horns are
    buffered bright.
And blood oozes through his white-linen gloves and his skin
    glows red in the night.
And his tail coils like an oily snake and the hellfires blaze in
    his eyes.
On those craggy rocks, he stands and blocks the way to paradise.
"Well, my, my, my, what have we here in my domain of sin?
In all my years as Prince of the Dark, it's the first case of
    anybody breaking m.
And of all the daredevil darin' dudes, well, who should the
    hero be?
But my old friend Billy Markham—who once made a punk
    out of me.
I heard you was in Heaven, Billy, humpin' angels all day long,
What's the matter—did God get sick to his stomach listening
    to your raunchy songs?
You made me the laughing stock of Hell, and the whole world
    laughed along with you.

Now here you come crashin' my party again:

Now tell me, just who's devilin' who?

Now, I didn't invite you down here, Bill, and nobody twisted
     your arm.

But you're back down here on my turf now, down here where
     it's cozy and warm.

So no more dice and no more games and no more jive stories
     to tell.

Just the Devil and a man with three souls in his hand dangling
     between Heaven and...

But, hey, what's this? Only *two*? Only *two* souls you've set
     free?

You must have forgot and left one behind: now who could
     that third one be?

Could it be your own true love, the one with the sweet wet
     smile?

The one you curse with each bitter breath 'cause she played
     with the Devil awhile?   ·

You call yourself free? Tee-hee, tee-hee. Why you prudish
     judgmental schmuck.

You'd leave your sweet love burn in Hell for one harmless
     little suck.

What would you rather she had done, leaped in the boiling
     manure...

So's you could keep your fantasy of someone sweet and pure?

She's a woman, flesh and bone, and they do what they do
     what they do.

And right or wrong, she needs no curse from a hypocrite like
    you.
So she shall rule with me—Billy Markham's love shall rule
    with me. She shall sit next to me on my throne.
And the whole world shall know—that the Devil's heart has
    more tenderness than your own.
So get your ass back up that rope, climb back to your
    promised land.
And hold your illusions of momma and daughter tight in your
    sweatin' hand.
But you'll see, you'll see, they're as human as she and you'll
    scream when you find it's true.
But please—stay up there and scream to God—Hell's gates
    are closed to you."
And Billy Markham, clutching his loves, climbs upward toward
    the skies.
And is it the sharp night wind that brings the tears to Billy's eyes?
Or is it the swirling sulfur smoke or the bright glare of the sun?
Or is it the sound of the wedding feast that the demons below
    have begun?

BILLY MARKHAM' S WEDDING

The trumpets of Hell have sounded the word like a screeching
    clarion call.

The trumpets of Hell have sounded the word and the word
    will be heard by all.
The trumpets of Hell have sounded the word and it reaches
    the heavenly skies.
Come angels, come demons, come dancing dead, the Devil is
    taking a bride.
And out of the Pearly Gates they come in a file two by two.
For when the Devil takes a bride, there's none that dare refuse.
And Jesus himself, he leads the way down through the starless
    night.
With the Mother Mary at his left side and Joseph on his right.
And then comes Adam and then comes Eve and the saints
    move close behind.
And all the gentle and all the good, in an endless column they
    wind.
Down, down to the pits of Hell, down from the heavens they
    sift—
Like fallen stars to a blood-red sea, each bearing the Devil a
    gift.
The strong and the brave, the halt and the lame, the deaf and
    the blind and the dumb.
And last of all comes Billy Markham, cursing the night as he
    comes.
Hell's halls are decked with ribbons of red and the feast has
    been prepared.
And the Devil and his bride sit side by side in skull-and-
    crossbone chairs.

And the Devil grins as his guests file in, for he is master now.
And one by one they enter his realm—and one by one they
    bow.
And the Devil whispers, "Thank you, friends," and he swells
    his chest with pride.
"Come give me your blessings and place your gifts at the feet
    of my blushing bride.
Lucrezia Borgia has made the punch of strychnine, wine, and
    gin.
And Judas has set the supper table on hallowed, bloody
    linen.
The feast is a human barbecue, and the sauce is beriberi,
Chopped up by Lizzie Borden and cooked by Typhoid Mary.
Here's some half-eaten apples from the Garden of Eden.

[*Offers bucket.*]

Here's some tidbits from Donner Pass.
Here's some fine old wine an acquaintance of mine
Made out of water, lemme fill your glass.
So you and you, drink of this crimson brew, we're all brothers
    and sisters under the skin.
And take off your costumes of virtue and sin, and
Let the revels begin."
And slowly and shyly they strip off their wings, and hide their
    halos away.
And they shyly touch hands—and begin to dance, as Hell's
    band begins to play.

There is Nero madly fiddlin' his fiddle, and Gabriel blowin'
    his horn.
And Idi Amin is beatin' his drum and Caligula's bangin' his gong.
Francis Scott Key plays piano and he's there 'cause he wrote
    that song.
And the pipes of Pan lead the Devil's band and everybody
    rocks along.
There's Janis and Elvis and Jimi and Cass, singin' them
    gimme some blues.
And Adolf Hitler and Joan of Arc start doin' the boogaloo.
Lady Godiva jumps off her horse, and Kate Smith starts
    shakin' her hips.
And the Marquis de Sade does a promenade laughin' and
    crackin' his whips.
Genghis Khan got a tutu on, and he's doing a pirouette,
When out of the cake with a wiggle and shake comes a naked
    Marie Antionette.
And King Farouk, he moons the crowd, while swingin' from
    the ceiling,
As Adam and the snake have one more drink just to show
    there's no hard feelings.
Isadora Duncan's getting' kind of drunk, and
Doin' something filthy with a scarf,
And they bring out the turkey, and Jack the Ripper says,
"Hey, I'll be glad to carve."
And there's old Dante dealing three-card Monte, Harpo Marx
    is tellin' jokes,

While Fatty Arbuckle is trying to collect the deposit on a
    bottle of Coke.
Elliot Ness shows up in a dress and Dillinger asks him to
    dance,
While Ivan the Terrible's tryin' to get into Susan B. Anthony's
    pants.
'N bare-ass naked on the balustrade sits Edgar Allan Poe,
Posin' for a two-dollar caricature by Michelangelo.
Abraham Lincoln and John Wilkes Booth, they're posin' for
    publicity photos,
While out in the foyer Richard the Third is comparing his
    hump with Quasimodo's.
And Catherine the Great, she's makin' a date with the horse
    of Paul Revere,
While Don Juan whispers love and lust into Helen Keller's ear.
And General MacArthur and Tokyo Rose, they're gigglin'
    behind the door,
While the daughters of Lot are yellin' "Hey, Pop, let's do it
    just once more."
And then John Wayne and Mary Magdalene announce
    they're going steady,
While Abel and Cain form a daisy chain with Jeannette
    McDonald and Nelson Eddy.
And Doctor Faust and Johann Strauss, Nabokov and Errol
    Flynn,
They're arguin' over some teenaged girl that they're all
    interested in.

Lee Harvey Oswald's tryin' to make a phone call, getting in
    some target practice,
And Salome's in the hall playin' volleyball with the head of
    John the Baptist.
And Al Capone gives Eva Braun a big bouquet of roses,
And Gertrude Stein has a little more wine and hits on
    Grandma Moses.
Delilah, she's clippin' and snippin' the snakes out of old
    Medusa's hair,
While Oscar Wilde says to Billy the Kid, "Can I show you
    'round upstairs?"
And the Devil, he sips his boilin' blood
And glances side to side
From the eyes of Billy Markham
To the eyes of his own sweet bride.
Then the music stops—and all heads turn—and the revelers
    freeze where they stand.
As Billy Markham approaches the throne and says, "May I
    have this dance?"
"And who be this?" the Devil snorts, "with the balls to think
    he can
Just walk up to the Devil's throne and ask the Devil's bride to
    dance?
Can this . . . can this be Billy Markham, who loves only the
    chaste and the pure?
No, Billy wouldn't bow and kiss the hand of a woman he once
    called whore.

But whoever this poor, lonely wretch may be, it is my
    wedding whim,
That no man be refused this day—step down, darlin', and
    dance with him."
The Devil grins and waves his tail, the music begins again
    gentle and warm.
As the lady nervously steps from her throne into Billy
    Markham's arms.
And the guests all snicker and snigger and wait, and they
    watch the dancers' eyes,
As 'round and 'round the floor they swirl 'tween Hell and
    Paradise.

[*Dances with mop.*]

"Oh, baby doll," says Billy Markham, "I've done you an awful
    wrong.
And to show you how rotten bad I feel, I even wrote about it
    in a song.
I never should have called you a dirty whore, and I never
    should have spit on your bed.
And I never should have left you to burn here in Hell 'cause
    you gave the Devil some head.
But if there's any hellish or heavenly way that I can make
    things right,
For your sweet sake, whatever it takes, I'll get you away
    tonight."

And the lady smiles a mysterious smile, as 'round the room
they swing,
And she whispers low in Billy's ear: "Well, there is…one little
thing."

Now the hall is empty, the guests are gone, and there on the
rusted throne,
Hand in hand in golden bands, the Devil and bride sit alone.
And the Devil stretches and yawns and grins, "Well, it has
been quite a day,
And now it's time to seal our love in the usual mortal way."
And the devil strips off his crimson cloak, and he casts the
pitchfork aside,
And he frees his oily two-pronged tail, and waits to take his
bride.
And his true love lifts her wedding dress up over her angel's
head.
And hand in hand they make their way to the Devil's fiery
bed.
And her upturned breasts glow warm in the fire, and her legs
are shapely and slim.
And for the very first time since time began, the Devil feels
passion in him.
"Now for the moment of truth," he whispers. "My love, my
queen, my choice."
"I love you, too, motherfucker," she laughs—in Billy
Markham's voice.

And the Devil leaps up and howls so loud that the fires of
    Hell blow cold.
"Ain't no big deal," says Billy's voice. "While we was dancing,
    we swapped souls.
Now she's up in Heaven singin' my songs and wearin' my
    body, too.
Safe forever in the arms of the Lord, while I'm down here in
    the arms of you."
"Why you creepin' crud," the Devil cries. "I'll teach you to
    fuck with my brain.
I'll give you a child who weighs ninety-five pounds, you
    wanna talk about screamin' pain!"
"Oh no, no, no," says Billy Markham. "I will be your wife
    only in name—
You come near me with that double-pronged dick, and I'll rip
    it right off of your frame."
"Shhhh…," says the Devil. "Not so loud. If Hell learns
    what's been done.
They'll laugh me off this golden throne and damn me to
    kingdom come.
And you—you've given me my true love's body with a
    hustler's soul inside.
You know more of torture than I've ever dreamed—you're fit
    to be my bride."
"Well, don't take it so hard," Billy Markham says. "You know
    things could be worse.
Havin' *her* soul in *my* body—now, that would be a curse.

But you and me, we got lots in common, we both like to
    shoot the shit.
And we both like to joke, and we both like to smoke, and we
    both like to gamble a bit.
And that should be the makin's for a happy marriage, and
    since neither one of us is gonna die,
Well, we might as well start the honeymoon—you wanna cut
    the cards or should I?"

Now the wedding night is a hundred years past and their
    garments have rotted to rags.
But face to face they sit in the flames, dealing five-card stud
    and one-eyed jacks.
And sometimes they play pinochle, sometimes they play gin.
And sometimes the Devil rakes in the pots, and sometimes
    the lady wins.
And sometimes they just sit and reminisce of the night they
first were wed.
From dawn to dawn the game goes on...
They *never* go to bed.

A. K. Abeille and
David Manos Morris

A Little Haunting

from

The Best American
Short Plays 2011–2012

setting

A girl's bedroom. Someone sleeping in the bed. Bedside table with lamp and book. Slippers on the floor.

[*At rise: A man falls backward into the room.*]

MAN   Sheesh! What—?

[*Spies person sleeping in the bed.*]

Oh! Cr—sh! Sh, sh, sh, sh—

[*Whispering.*]

—okay. Okay. Okay. I can do this. I can do this.

[*Pulls out a piece of paper.*]

I just have to successfully haunt each client, and I can move up to bigger and better locations. How hard can it be? Some little girl. No sweat. Who knew that the afterlife would have ghost middle managers giving out assignments. I screamed "BOOO!" in his face. Priceless. No one's ever told me what to do before, and I don't take their crap in the afterlife either.

[*Creeps over to look at the sleeper, then whispers back toward the way he came in.*]

No problem. This'll be better than dumping little Kyle Kosinski in the trash and stealing his pants. She'll be cryin' for momma in ten seconds. I'll be haunting movie stars and politicians in no time. Watch this!

[*Starts stalking around the bed, waving his arms weirdly.*]

Oooooooo. Ooowooooooo! Boooooooooooo! BoooooOOOOOOOOoooooo.

[*No response from sleeper.*]

Sound sleeper.

[*Looks around; takes the book from the bedside table and "floats" it around the room and over the bed.*]

Oooooooo. Oh, OOOOOOOOOO! Boo. Boo, kid. Dang. What, your parents NyQuil you or something? What!

[*He drops the book on the floor with a thump; no response from sleeper.*]

Okay, okay—I get it, I pissed you off, you give me narcoleptic-girl. No problem. Up the game.

[*Looks around; jumps for the lamp; tries to turn it on but can't find the switch.*]

Wh—crud.

[*Picks up the lamp and hovers it over the bed.*]

Little girl—little girl! Want a lamp on your—

[*Notices the lamp cord just trails, no plug on the end.*]

Great; no wonder it doesn't work. Duh. What's the matter, you reading too late, Mommy Dearest cut the cord?

[*Flips the lamp around over the sleeper's head a few times, moaning, mimes about to smash her with it in frustration.*]

Wow, are you a heavy sleeper or what?

[*Puts lamp back; spies the book on the floor, picks it up.*]

Must be one heck of a bedtime story.

[*Tries to open the book, but it is made of wood.*]

What the—? What kind of parents—? Not your business, spook! You're the haunt—haunt!

[*Ditches the book; creeps up near the bed, starts shaking the covers, then the bed itself.*]

Hauuuuuunting! Haaaaaaaaaunting! I'm haaaaunting you, little girl!

[*Shouting.*]

You're haunted!

[*No response from sleeper.*]

For Pete's sake!

[*Violently shaking the bed.*]

Wake up! Wake up! No way. No way! She's dead? She's *dead*?! That's not fair. That's not *fair*! Nobody can wake the—noooo way...

[*He backs away from the bed, hits the wall—tries to get out of the room the way he came in, then tries the other walls, increasingly desperate.*]

Hey! Hey, let me out of here! Manager dude! Crap, man! Get me the—get me out of here! You can't stick me in here with a dead girl and I can't get out until I can scare her! Nobody can! Hey!

[*He gives up, panting, then pulls out his contract again, scanning it quickly.*]

…mission support! There!

[*He pulls out a cell phone and makes a call.*]

I want to speak to a manager. There's something wrong with my assignment.

[*He pauses until his boss comes on the phone.*]

Hey, to you too. Get me another client right now. You screwed up, and I'm not going to take the crap for this. No way. No way. Yeah, I know the contract says I can't move on until I scare the "present client"—but you don't get it! She's already dead or something. She's dead! She's *dead*, you idiot! I don't know, crib death or something. No, she's not a baby, I just mean—she's just lying there—died in her sleep or something—she—what? What do you mean the client's just fine and hasn't been scared at all? Hasn't been scared, man, she's frickin' dead over here!

I'll go over your head. I'll have your job. You can't stick me with this client. That's not fair! That's not *fair*! Nobody can wake the—Wait, she can't hear me! Is that it? That's the deal, isn't it? She's deaf, is that it? Some equal opportunity haunting bullshit? Oh, fine. Think I feel sorry for poor little deafy girl and won't give her a real haunt? Think you're gonna stop me moving up by giving me some pity case? Idiot. I'll be your boss this time tomorrow. Listen to this!

[*Goes over to the bed, but hears the manager cut off the call.*]

Hello? Hello? Idiot.

Whatever. Here you go, deafo!

[*Shakes the mattress violently, then turns the mattress clear over, spilling sleeper out.*]

WAKE UP!

[*Sleeper is clearly a doll.*]

A doll.

[*Relieved.*]

It's just a doll—she's not dead, she's just a d—Wait a minute. You said I had to—how could I—okay, that really isn't fair! I can't scare a little girl that *isn't* even—

WOMAN'S VOICE [*Offstage.*]   Lana? Have you got everything you want to put in storage?

GIRL'S VOICE [*Offstage.*]   Just about—I just want to bring the dollhouse; I need more room for my new stereo!

MAN   [*Looks around frantically, putting the pieces together.*] *Dollhouse*?! Wait—! [*Loses his balance as the house is lifted.*] Wait! Wait! Booo! BoooooOOOOOOO!

WOMAN'S VOICE [*Offstage.*]   Oh, someday when you have a little girl of your own, she's going to treasure this.

MAN   When she has—hey, I can't wait until this little *girl* has a kid! WAIT! BOOOOOOOO!

GIRL'S VOICE [*Offstage.*]   Mom! I think we might have mice in the walls again! I hear that squeaking. . .

WOMAN'S VOICE [*Offstage.*]   Oh no—I'll call the exterminator right away; just put that right in this box honey and tape it up tight . . .

[*Man falls over the doll, still protesting, as blackout.*]

Jean-Claude van Itallie
and Joseph Chaikin

Struck Dumb

from

The Best American
Short Plays 1991–1992

Notes from an Author of *Struck Dumb*

Joe Chaikin and I have been close friends and co-workers in
the theater since 1963 when Joe founded and directed the
Open Theater, of which I was the principal playwright.

In May of 1984 Joe suffered a stroke during heart surgery
to repair a faulty valve. As a result of this stroke, Joe became
aphasic. His speech and comprehension of speech became
"out of phase."

I wrote a play, *The Traveller*, inspired by experiences around
Joe's stroke, which premiered in Los Angeles at the Mark Taper
Forum in the spring of 1987. During rehearsals I thought it
would be useful for Joe to have a play to perform himself along
with the short *War in Heaven*, which Joe and Sam Shepard had
written before and just after Joe's stroke.

Gordon Davidson and Madeline Puzo at the Taper were
kind enough to commission *Struck Dumb*, and we started writing

while Joe and I and the dramaturge Bill Coco were living close to where our character, Adnan, lives in Venice, California.

Struck Dumb is a play about an aphasic character, who may be played by an aphasic actor needing to read his lines rather than memorize them. Adnan, in the middle of his life, is newborn to language and to the world.

Struck Dumb is a theatrical metaphor for Adnan's mind. Adnan's written thoughts appear to him from all parts of the stage.

It is Joe's hope and mine that *Struck Dumb* will focus attention on the problems and potentials of persons afflicted with aphasia. There are about a million aphasics in the United States. The very nature of aphasia requires a voice.

It has been said that one does not usually recover from aphasia, but that, by dint of hard work and time, one recovers *with* aphasia.

—Jean-Claude van Itallie
Boulder, Colorado
March 14, 1989

character

Adnan

scene

Venice, California. Time: 1988

[*Facing the audience, on an old oriental carpet, is a comfortable chair and a wooden desk, with a monitor, a tape deck, and a typewriter. Some of the objects have hand-lettered signs on them saying what they are: "desk" and "tapes."*]

[ADNAN, *who is aphasic, may be played by an aphasic actor who cannot memorize lines but who can read them.* ADNAN *may also be played by a nonaphasic actor who does not ever lapse into speaking memorized lines.*]

[*The production provides a spare, functional set as well as a changing environment of text and light, which helps* ADNAN *from place to place on the stage (as if he were going from home to seashore to Santa Monica mall to sunset on the pier).*]

[ADNAN *is sometimes surprised by his own thoughts when the text appears suddenly on a placard or is lit on a floor-to-ceiling scroll (giving mosque-like overtones to the set).*]

[*Some music and sound may be used, but the principal focus is the actor's voice. During the course of the play, the light changes from dawn to night.*]

WAKING UP

[ADNAN, *fifty-ish, is in his "home" area of the stage, behind his desk. He wears comfortable clothing (with may be a slight middle-Eastern flavor). He does not look poor or alien. As he leans back, the first text comes down to him suddenly from the ceiling on a placard.*]

Waking up: it's a shock.
Sleeping: it's dreaming, it's traveling, it's easy. But waking,
Waking up on earth, it's amazing.
Every morning: an event.

Every morning, ordinary.
I look, wanting to find "perfect."
But there is no "perfect."
Except sometimes—
A few seconds—they are perfect.

Every, every day, waking:
I wonder, what is this room?
What is this day?
What planet?
Light?
Lights?
Sky?
Only one sun?
How to move this body?
Body: it's universe.

Sometimes feeling—it's tremor—
It's trauma—
Starting small, sometimes from nothing—
Trembling: starting tiny, tiny like tic.
Look at my face, look: tic.

[*He shows a tic on his face.*]

Then twitch.

[*His tic becomes bigger.*]

Tic becomes a twitch. And then quiver.

[*His tic becomes even bigger.*]

And then shudder. Shudder.

[*His whole body starts to shake.*]

And tremor. Tremor. Tremor.

[*His body shakes more.*]

And then shake, and shake, and then—

[*He is still.*]

And then what?

I have a fear of…what?

[*ADNAN listens. He has a few characteristic emblematic movements, such as the way he holds his head as he listens for an earthquake, as he does now.*]

It's difficult to hear.
Like a blind person, needing to imagine colors—
Listening in the blindness.

[*He listens again.*]

Feeling, trembling.
Not once, but maybe twenty-five times.
Every day: earthquake.
Cataclysm…
It's crisis in universe, stars, planets…
Crisis causing changing, of course.
So what is changing?
Changing, it's "evolving."
Even thinking about changing, it's change.

MY HOUSE

My name is Adnan.
I was born in Beirut, in Lebanon,
In a big house.
Beirut, it's an ancient city.
Lebanon, my country,
Five thousand years ago,
It was called Phoenicia.

Now I am living in Venice, California.
I have a bedroom and a kitchen.

It's morning; I have coffee, and then breakfast:
Toast of something.
I'm eating something—it's a muffin.

It's "taste." I'm amazed—
Shock.

[ADNAN *listens.*]

Tremor, quake—it's shaking again.
Earth groaning again.

[ADNAN *listens, then returns to normal.*]

This room has only three or four things.
Simple, it's better, it's best.

This is my desk. It's wood.
The desk exists longer than I am human,
Longer than my father, longer than my grandfather.
It's from the Shakers.

These are my tapes.
Music, it's pulse and rhythm and melody.
I see music.
My greatest pleasure, it's music: hearing God.

Then, second, it's colors.
I have pleasure also from shapes—like shells, from the sea.
Music, it might be shapes.
Thinking about shapes, shells.
Bodies—
Like air, like clouds...
For example, spiders—many legs, many arms.

Spider to galaxy, spinning...spiral.
Shapes...

[ADNAN *gestures a spiral shape.*]

This is my clock. It's new.
Time—oh, yes—it's important to me now,
It's order.
Without clock, one second or one year—no different.
But when I leave my house,
When I go to the ocean,
When I'm looking at the sea,
I do not want a clock at all.

THE SEA

[ADNAN *walks toward the "beach" area of the stage.*]

Here, it's just an ordinary place, Venice.
But—on the sea,
And you have to be living someplace.

I was living in Paris once.
I was a student, learning about the voice.
And then I was singing.
I sang concerts many times.
And then: cataclysm, expulsion:
I was struck dumb.

[ADNAN *listens.*]

I am obsessed about earthquake.
Some people have obsess about ice cream,
Or drugs, or sex.
With me: it's earthquake.

[ADNAN *listens.*]

I am thinking about this and that—
And then, after two minutes, again—

[ADNAN *listens. Then* ADNAN *walks.*]

Many refugees come to the beach,
Many refugees come speaking French.
I was speaking French when I was three.
Refuse—refugees—
Coming to the beach like tide, waves…

Jean-Paul Sartre, he's my friend.
I never met him really.
He's short.
He's ghost.
Before, I was never thinking about ghost at all.
But now, thinking about ghost a lot.
Thinking myself ghost.
Well, not myself,
But ghost using my voice maybe.

[ADNAN *makes a ghostly sound.*]

I don't speak so well now,
So why ghost choosing my voice?
I don't know. It's mysterious.
Ghost, it's funny.

[*ADNAN walks.*]

Walking on street to ocean every day.
Going outside, I look back at my house:
It's yellow and gray;
It's thin and small;
It's not perfect.
But it's only two blocks from the sea.
If I could have a different house,
I would live in the sea.
My room, it's small.
The sea, it's enormous.

Every day, walking down the street to the sea,
I pick a leaf from the same bush.
Every day.
I don't know why.
Every day I taste the leaf.
The taste is bitter:
It's shock to my body.
Earthquake, it's shock to Mother Earth.

[ADNAN *listens.*]

Listen.

[ADNAN *listens.*]

I'm listening all the time.
Someone told me once:
Everything everybody ever said
Is still out there in the universe vibrating.
Listen.
It's ghosts' voices vibrating:
Ghosts shuddering, moving, hovering.

[ADNAN *walks.*]

Every day, on the street,
I meet a dog.
I'm looking into her eyes.
She's looking at me.

[ADNAN *looks as if at a dog.*]

She's cute: a thousand curlies, her hair.
It's golden and it's brown,
Like cashew, the nut.
She's not my dog really, but almost.
Her name is Cashew.
Not really, but I love the name "Cashew."
Cashew's happy to see me.

[ADNAN *is greeting the dog.*]

Hello. Hi, Cashew, hi.
She's jumping, she's happy.
But animals not thinking.
Cashew, she's smart.
And she's graceful.
Like a ballet dancer,
But she's not thinking at all.
Animals do not drink tea, or coffee, like humans.
Animals are different.

Thinking, it's humans'…
Humans' what?
What is thinking?
No answer.

What is endless… endless… endless?
Eternity—what is it?
No answer.

When body is finished,
What happens to soul?

No answer.

Is something continuing?
What is it?

No answer.

Does Cashew have a soul also?
No answer.

Before, I didn't know I had a soul.
Now that I know, what to do?
What to do with my soul?

I am like: "Man struck dumb after writing letter to God."
Writing: "Dear God, I'm tired of my life.
Please send me something new."
So God strikes him dumb.

It's dangerous, writing a letter to God.
You sometimes get what you want.

People in Venice don't work much.
Everybody's bum, or retired.

My name is Adnan.
I was born in Beirut, in Lebanon.
Once I was a singer.
Now myself, I could be—what?
Orchestra conductor?
Guide to Zoo?
Prince of Wales?
Astronomer?
Deep-sea diver?
Dope dealer?
Weatherman?
Foster father?

Actually, I am now a philosopher.
It does not pay well.
I am a philosopher, but I have no answers.
You must live without answers.
I want to know things clearly.
The questions must be clear.
But I must live without answers.

[ADNAN *walks.*]

Walking on sand,
Just thinking, touching on things:
Where land meets water—it's boundary.

The poor and the rich,
Everybody walks on the beach.

There is more sea than land.
Myself, I'm mostly water, like the ocean.
Myself, I'm a mammal.

If I am slippery in this lifetime—
I could be reborn a whale.
Maybe myself already born many times whale,
Living in ocean, my home.

[ADNAN *touches the water.*]

Water.
This is cold water touching my hand. It's shock.

[*A placard comes in quickly on a pulley, accompanied by a loud grinding sound.*]

Water!
Ocean spilling,
Earth, it's splitting, it's cracking,
Ocean, it's spilling,
Earth's face, it's splitting,
Earth brain, it's cracking open.

[ADNAN *breathes hard. Then he is back to normal.*]

The sea is like mother.
French word "mother," sounds the same as the word for sea:
Mer, it's sea, and mother—
It's deep, the ocean.
Nobody knows exactly what's down there.

PRACTICING WORDS

[ADNAN *goes back to his desk. He turns on the tape machine, leans back in his chair, listening to classical music. We watch him listen. When the music is over, he reaches for his word cards on his desk.*]

I am practicing words.
"Sugar and salt"—it's flowers and metal.
"Astonishing": it's a word, an explosion.
"My," it's a funny word:

"My" clock. "My" house. "My" word.

And "meaning."

"Meaning," it's a huge word.

To choose a word—it's a choice.

Turning this way, that.

Repetition, repetition: "life," "living," "live," "SHOCK."

And another word: "conscious."

"Unconscious" and "conscious."

And "mysterious."

Anything to do with speech, it's work. "Abandon": it's a word.

I want to abandon it.

And "evolving":

It's another word for dying.

"Evolving": it happens.

And word "ghost," it's like "guest," and "goats."

Other words: "extreme," "hate,"

"Jealous," "curse," "vengeance," "anguish,"

"Terror," "mourning," and then: "rapture."

And then "galaxies!" Oh.

So my face is my words.

[ADNAN *looks at the audience.*]

Look my face. Here it is.

[*He shrugs.*]

THE LETTER

[ADNAN *holds a letter.*]

I have a friend.
Before, I didn't know her well.
But since we are both struck by lightning,
She's family to me.
Her name is Diane.
She's 'phasic, like me.

You know, "aphasia"?
It's another word.
It's Greek.
Tragedy.
And some comic.

I like to laugh.
Laughing, it's "infectious."

Listen.
It's a letter.
It's a letter to me.

[ADNAN *reads the letter.*]

"My dear friend. You ask me to tell you what happened to me twelve years ago. It's a long time, twelve years. Since my accident. I remember being hit by a car—feeling it bounce off me. Then it was coma. It was coma for five weeks. They were not sure I'd wake up. I don't remember anything. You know coma, coma—it's nothing—it's just a hole. Before I was a model, about pictures. I was a famous model. Isn't that strange? One day: an accident, and I woke up part of the aphasia family."

[*He stops reading.*]

It's true.
Diane, she's family.
Rest of world—it's abstract to me, it's chaos.
It's Greek again: "chaos."
Universe starting from chaos.
Beginning everything, it's chaos,
Coming from water,
Coming to civilization.
Greek: it's islands, from earthquake.
Aphasia, it's chaos again.
Chaos, it's changing direction suddenly.
From nowhere, left becoming right,
Right becoming left:
Switching—confusion suddenly.
It's chaos?
It's civilization?
Which?

Listen, my mind, I have a question.
What is real—
Universe or stage?

Now thinking about planets and earth.
And now: especially theater.

So here we are.

[ADNAN *looks at the audience.*]

I'm listening.
Now I'm going to tell a story about ghosts.

[*At his desk, his face is lit eerily by the monitor from which he reads the text.*]

I'm haunted by ghosts.

Ghost has nothing to do with time.
We have different time from ghost.
Ghost has no substance.

Ghost trembles.
Ghost vibrates fast.
Ghost disappears.
It comes,
It goes.
Maybe it's reborn.
Ghost lives in this world
Because there is only this world.
But maybe ghost goes to other planets.

It's mysterious...
Ghosts hovering...
A ghost doesn't need to dwell in a house.
A ghost is hovering.

If a ghost speaks inside your head,
Do you obey that ghost?
I am rebellious.
I argue with the ghost.

Jean-Paul Sartre, he says to me:
"Adnan, whooo, whooo,
Keep your mind on the ball.
Stop dreaming, whooo, whooo.
Adnan, stake your life to *something*, whooo, whooo.
Commit yourself, Adnan, whooo, whooo."
"To what, Jean-Paul?
To what should I stake my life?"
But Jean-Paul, he just says, "Whooo, whooo . . ."
And then, he flies away.
He's funny, Jean-Paul.

One ghost—she's a woman I knew thirty years ago—her
        name is Susan Dye.
She died from a brain tumor.
Surgeons put dye right in her brain.
I don't understand that.
Her brain, it turned red.

She had so much pain.
Sometimes, Susan Dye, the ghost,
Talks to me through the pain in my neck.
I'm thinking about the neck.
When a wolf loses a fight with another wolf,
He exposes his neck.
It's vulnerable, the neck.

[ADNAN *stretches his neck, approaching it with his hand as if with a knife.*]

One touch, and that's it.

THE MALL

[*Slightly comical, simple music as* ADNAN *walks to the "mall" part of the stage.*]

Every afternoon walking Santa Monica, the mall.
What's meaning, the word "mall"?
It's street?
On the street—I'm looking at everyone's face.

[ADNAN *examines the audience.*]

It's incredible, faces.

[ADNAN *sees the violinist.*]

One guy, he's playing music.
It's violent—no, it's violin.
"Violin" and "violent," it's similar.
You see, I can't talk well—
He's wanting money in cup.
He's flat in the key of violin.
But later I find myself walking back,
And giving him two dollars.
I don't know why.
It was Mozart.

[ADNAN *walks*.]

California, really, it's funny.

One person is talking, talking, talking,
Babble, babble, babble,
And the other person is answering, always "Hmm."

[*He nods his head, as if responding.*]

"Hmm."
"Babble, babble…"
"Hmm. Hmm. Great, great."
"Babble, babble."
"Hmm. Hmm. Great, great."
"Babble, babble."
"Hmm. Great, great."

[ADNAN *shrugs.*]

It's funny.

[ADNAN *points.*]

She her, see her over there?
She's young.
She's not beautiful, but almost: pretty.
One day a guy, rich, maybe banker,
Coming sexually to her: "Hello."
And she's smiley, "Hello,"
And puts her hand on his shoulder,
And a hand around his waist:
She's taking his wallet!
It's true.
I saw it.
She's pickpocket!

Sometimes, myself wanting to shout on street,
Like crazy person:
"Earth, it's beautiful,
Earth, it's too beautiful.
Watch out, watch out!
Earth, it's dangerous."
But shouting to whom?
To you, my friends.
Who else?

Through the pastry window, I see the cook.
He's working there at the oven.
The cook and myself.
We wave through glass,
But we never talk.

That man and that woman
Do not see me.
They are looking in the window of a store.
He calls her Lisa.
Lisa is talking, talking, talking.
Lisa is a liar. I see lying in her face.
Lisa lies so much
She forgets she is lying.
Meanwhile her friend is daydreaming.
His fantasy: to live in the jungle,
To be Tarzan.
But really he works in an office.

What's a curse?
A curse means you are stuck.
You will never be different,
Never grow,
Never change from right now.
That's a curse.

I love to eat.
I like eating in Ethiopian restaurant

With my friends.
Many people's conversation to me, it's babble, of course
—Like Tower of Babble—
But I like to listen
By watching faces.

I have a friend.
His name is Fred Graves.
It's a serious name.
It's dark.
He could be Fred Dark,
Fred Coffin,
Fred Catastrophe,
Fred Cataclysm,
Or Fred Earthquake.
But he's very happy, really.
He's coming from satellite—
No—I mean Seattle. Seattle.
But now, Fred, he's living in Venice.
Telling Fred: I'm scared of dying.
Freddy, he says to me:
"Adnan, it's not so bad,
So die, already."
It's good advice.
Fred, he's funny.

[ADNAN *walks.*]

SUNSET

Some days, going home,
Seeing sunset from pier,
And seagulls flying.

[ADNAN *listens.*]

I'm listening.
It's evening.
Light.
Lights.
Stars.
Sky.
And seagulls flying.

[ADNAN *listens.*]

I'm listening.
It's new to me,
Watching stars.
Planets, for instance:
There are no numbers...the planets...endless...
Like atoms in a piece of shell.
Violently born, the stars—they must be.
Earth born violently:
Everything swirling.
Universe born violently.

It's not so sweet—
Not like California hangaround.
I relish some violence in myself.
Maybe planets inside yourself—myself.
Planet, it's like light from inside.
It's Venus, Mercury, Saturn...

[ADNAN *listens.*]

Earth ending—it's going to happen when?
Earth, it's five billion years old.
Myself five billion years old.

[*ADNAN listens.*]

Earth, it's happening again.
I'm listening.
She's throbbing.
Can you feel, she's throbbing?

[ADNAN *shakes.*]

Earth the Mother, she's trembling,
And everyone behaving like it's not happening.
But animals, really animals, they know.
Oh, yes.
When earthquake coming—before—
All animals running away.
Running north.
It's true.

[ADNAN *listens.*]

I'm listening.
It's mysterious.
I am living in water,
In air,
On earth,
And sun is fire.

Planets, stars...
Planets are on and on...
Like seagulls flying...
On and on...
Endless...Stars...
Sky...
You know, it's really endless...
Endless...
More than possible to imagining...
On and on...
On and on...
On and on...
On and on...
On...

[*Lights out.*]

Part II

Monologues
for Women

Mac Wellman

excerpts from

The Sandalwood Box

from

The Best American
Short Plays of 1995–1996

setting

In the rain forest of South Brooklyn.

PROFESSOR CLAUDIA MITCHELL   [*A professor of
cataclysm at Great Wind University.*] This is…

[*She holds up a small, bright object.*]

Seoul, Korea. December 25th, 1971. The worst hotel fire in
history. An eight-hour blaze at the 222-room Taeyokale
Hotel. A total of 163 persons are incinerated or succumb to
the horrors of noxious inhalation. Two workmen are later
sent to prison for terms of three to five years, convicted of
carelessness in the handling of gasoline.

[Pauses. She replaces it in its place and holds up another.]

This is Clontarf, Ireland, in the year 1014 AD. Danish raiders under chieftain Sweyn the First (Forkbeard) are repelled by the forces of King Brian Boru. The Danes are mauled, with a loss of 6,000, and driven back to their stumpy ships. Both Boru and his son are killed. Forkbeard is slain later that year. And another. Saint Gotthard Pass, Italian Alps. 1478. During the private war between the Duke of Milan and another feudal lord, an array of sixty stout Zurichers, allies of the Milanese, are flattened by an avalanche in the early afternoon, with the solar furnace blazing away so innocently above. And another. Kosovo, in former Yugoslavia. 1389. Prince Lazar's Serbian army of 25,000 meets the Spahis and Janizaries of Sultan Murad in the morning mists of the 28th of June. In accordance with a prophecy of the Unseen, the entire Serbian force is annihilated, thus clearing the way for Turkish mastery of the region for over half a millennium. And another. The Johnstown Flood. May 31, 1889. A wall of water thirty to forty feet high bursts down upon the town as the entire damn collapses. Over two thousand people are drowned, or dragged to their deaths over tree branches, barbed wires, and overturned houses. Victims continue to be unearthed, some far upstream, for the next seventeen years. Yet another. The retreat of the French Army from Moscow, begun on October 19th, 1812. Hounded cruelly by marauding Russian guerrillas, the Grande Armée is soon mangled, and beaten—

reduced to a desperate, starving horde. Snows begin to fall on November 4. Ten days later, Napoleon is left with only 25,000 able-bodied fighters. At the River Berezina 10,000 stragglers are abandoned in the crossing on the 29th. French losses are the worst in history: 400,000 men, 175,000 horses, 1,000 cannon.

[*Pause.*]

This wonderful collection constitutes only a merest part of the world catastrophe, which in toto comprises the dark side of the Unseen's id.

• • •

MARSHA GATES   [*A student and prop girl at Great Wind Repertory Theater.*] Why is the night better than the day? Why do the young become old, and not the other way around? Why is the world made mostly of clay? Why can't a person always tell what is wrong from what is right? Why does the full weight of the Unseen fall most heavily upon the visible, like brass? Why can't we see what it is that compels both cause and effect to be so interfixed? Why can't I find a number beyond which nothing can be enumerated? Why can't I know what will come of what I do, think, and say? Why can't I know truth from lies the way I do "up" from "down." Why is one person's disaster not catastrophe for all? And who knows why these things are called unaccounted.

Unaccountable. Uncountable. And why, oh why, don't we know who does know the answers to these things?

[*Pause.*]

. . . because isn't it so that if we possess, and are possessed by, a question, the answer must too be hidden somewhere, somewhere in the heart of someone, someone real, and not a phantom of the Unseen.

Darren Canady

excerpt from

You're Invited!

from

The Best American
Short Plays 2010–2011

setting

An upscale kitchen in an upscale home.

MAGGIE   [*Pointing out the window.*] Look! Look at 'em!

[*We hear the children brightly singing "Happy Birthday." As the kids keep singing.*]

Oh my God, look at 'em. They're pattin' Logan on the back, givin' him high fives and stuff. Wow! Hugs and kisses—the whole nine yards. Like they're actually having fun. Isn't that just like kids? The second we leave 'em alone, they actually start acting like humans. Like seriously. My Brian was a real dumbass the whole car ride over here. And he was like Mikey's lead cheerleader with the cake. But look at him now. I think Brian just kissed Logan on the forehead. He only acts likes an ass when I'm around. I think it's on purpose.

Kyle John Schmidt

excerpt from

St. Matilde's Malady

from

The Best American
Short Plays 2010–2011

setting

A private sitting room on the top floor of a massive preindustrial brothel.

MOLLY FORGE   [*A young prostitute.*] He was my evening's final customer. And he fell asleep astride me, my breasts rocking in the soft hammock of his palms, my hair entangled his, his eyes locked upon mine. We bedded our armies in blissful concordance. When we awoke, he called me his star fire, I lauded him my saintly fox. Then a thousand joyful kisses without purpose or monetary remuneration. I saw my life's end on the ruby curve of his lips and he said as much to me. It was right then that my hands froze into the puppets you see now. [...] Yes. He gave me St. Matilde's Malady. The moment he saw my hands, he bolted out of bed discovering that he couldn't bend his knees from a similar and simultaneous disease. Frightened, he robed himself to leave, dropping his oil tanker's wheel keys. I tried halting him, but limping so to travel farther, he trundled out my window and down the trumpet vines toward the harbor. [...] I hate him with all the darkness and fury caught in the monstrous hurricane of my soul. In a night he has caught my dear profession from these hands and abused the morning so he can steal away. If I ever see him again, I will use every fist my body can create to tear holes across his corpse. [...] Bullets of rain, calamity, thunder, wind whirl, and strike! I am the worst beast the wharf ever dreamed. My staid wooden dock demonically rises plank by plank from its stale marine home and writhes viciously high above the oceanic horizons. I am the storm tornadoes flee from. I am the bluster cities bow towards. I am the devil fire no virgin sea could dream.

John Bolen

excerpt from

A Song for Me, or Getting the Oscar

from

The Best American Short Plays 2010–2011

setting

The den of a small house in Venice, California.

EMMY   [*Late twenties to mid-thirties singer.*] Don't you remember we were pretty drunk when we got together that first time, and we were making love, and when I first saw your erection I accidentally blurted out, "Oh my, Oscar, look at you!" You asked me what I was saying, and I just quickly covered by saying I was referring to your penis as Oscar. I think I mumbled something like it was a little golden statuette. Well, after that, it was you that kept referring to it as Oscar, saying things like "Oscar wants attention." And "Oscar's feeling lonely tonight." And "Emmy's going to get the Oscar tonight." I couldn't stop you, you just kept going on and on about Oscar this and Oscar that. […] It just happened, Jake. But look at it this way. We spent that night together and every night after. And we've been married for five years and have our beautiful son, Sam, together. It really worked out for the best, didn't it?

Gabriel Rivas Gomez

excerpt from

Scar Tissue

from

The Best American
Short Plays 2010–2011

setting

The then and there, the here and now. USC Medical Center.

CLAUDIA   [*Heart surgeon, fifties. Attractive. Cold.*] The da
Vinci Robot can allow us to perform complicated procedures.
As you can see, this procedure is dramatically less invasive
than standard BACG, and as a result requires far less recovery
time. The da Vinci Surgical System allows a surgeon to get a
closer view of the heart and mimics the surgeon's movements.

[ALMA *demonstrates.*]

In addition, it compensates for minor, involuntary motions
which would otherwise make the procedure impractical. In
addition to controlling the arms, the surgeon can also control
the scope of his or her view. "Zoom." […] The most difficult

part of the procedure is the attachment of the blood vessel to the aorta. While the standard procedure allows the surgeon to use her hands to sew the tissue together, the da Vinci model uses a different method.

[*She demonstrates.*]

It punctures a small hole, here, and anchors the vessel similar to how a small rivet would work. [...] You'll notice the heart is still beating. This procedure, in most cases, is performed off pump, which is ultimately safer for the patient. What's more, the surgeon doesn't even need to be in the same room as the surgery. He can perform the procedure from his office with other attendees in the O.R. [...] This is the future, ladies and gentlemen. [...] In ten years, standard coronary bypass will be obsolete.

[CLAUDIA *sets her instruments down. She moves about the crowd with each question.*]

While the da Vinci machine is not cheap, we can expect to recover costs in twelve to fifteen months, at which point, it actually becomes a very cost-effective procedure. [...] The recovery time with this procedure is cut by 25 percent. What's more, since it is performed on a beating heart, the patient does not need to rely on a heart and lung bypass machine. As you know, the use of these machines has been called into question as some studies have shown a correlation between them and long-term depression. [...] We are in a result-oriented profession, doctor. If the patient lives, we have succeeded. If not, we've failed. So far, nineteen surgeries have been performed with the da Vinci machine. Zero have died. In fact, all of them have recovered at an extraordinary rate. We are not motivational speakers or therapists. We are not kindergarten teachers or priests. We are not paid to be peoples' friends. We are paid to do what most other people can't do: save lives. And this robot does that incredibly efficiently. I've selected the twentieth Da Vinci patient. You are welcome to observe. Once you do, I think you will agree that this machine should be a fixture at USC Medical.

Craig Pospisil

excerpts from

Dissonance

from

The Best American
Short Plays 2010–2011

setting

A room in a funeral home used for memorial services.

TRICIA   [*Early thirties.*] A good memory. Summer between junior and senior years at college I was s'posed to go to Europe with my dad, but he cancelled. Seems he'd just met the very beautiful, young, and soon-to-be second Mrs. Roberts, so he decided to take her instead. You'd think I'd've been mad at *him* for being stuck in Pittsfield all summer—and I was—but he wasn't around, so I took it out on my mom instead.

[*Slight pause.*]

I think she knew why I was being such a jerk, though, because she took me everywhere that summer. Museums, theater at Williamstown, minor-league baseball games. But my favorite was taking picnic dinners to Tanglewood for concerts like yours. And James Taylor. [...] By the time I went back to school we'd relapsed to our standard mother-daughter cat fights.

[*Pause.*]

By the next summer she'd been diagnosed. She thought she was being forgetful because she wasn't getting enough sleep. Oh, we had a good time. It was a beautiful night. Warm. Lying on a blanket and watching the stars overhead, while Debussy drifted through the air.

• • •

TRICIA   For years, while she got worse and worse, I was here every weekend. And it wasn't easy. I'm in Manhattan. I don't have a car. I'd ride four hours on a bus, get into town late Friday night, stay in a dingy hotel, then Saturday get a cab to Stony Field. Sometimes she knew me, and we'd fight. Sometimes she didn't know me, and we'd fight. Sometimes she knew me, and she'd cry. Sometimes she didn't know me, and I'd cry. Then I got to turn around and spend another five or six hours getting back home.

[*Pause.*]

I left angry and upset, and she forgot I'd even been there as soon as I left the room. Then one trip home I found myself wishing she'd just die. Wanting her to die.

[*Pause.*]

So I just stopped going. [...] I was at LAX just about ready to board a plane when they called to tell me she died. I was too stunned to do anything but just get on the plane to come home.

[*Slight pause.*]

I got bumped up to first class. Isn't that something? I travel a lot for work, and I'd just gotten enough frequent flyer miles to make the Silver Medallion class of membership. And I got upgraded. It was like they knew. I sit down and they give me a hot towel, which I press to my face, let the warmth sink into my skin. Then they bring me a mimosa. And when I finish that one...they bring another. And a third. Then somewhere over Nebraska...I snap. And I get up in the aisle and start tearing my clothes off, telling everyone on the plane what a terrible daughter I am because my mother who I haven't seen in five months just died alone.

Lisa Soland

excerpt from

Spatial Disorientation

from

The Best American
Short Plays 2012–2013

character

CAROLYN   John's wife, thirty-three, cocaine-addled.

time

July 16, 1999, at 8:00 p.m.

place

Essex County Airport in Fairfield Township, N.J.

setting

The moon has just risen above the horizon but barely casts
any light onto the ladder, which can be seen off in the distance,

upstage left, representing the steps one must take to board JFK Junior's private plane.

CAROLYN   I had to give up my job because of this, because of you. A job that I really enjoyed. And now it's gone and there's nothing. There's not a single place I can go without insufferable harassment, and you, the thing I left my job for...you work night and day, continuously, on and on and on. What do you expect me to do? What do you want me to do with my time, tell me? [...] A person can imagine, but really, John, this is impossible. The press is impossible. They followed me to the salon, seven or eight cars, snapping, flashes, riding my tail, trying to get me to falter, show my imperfection, finally getting that priceless photo of me flipping them off. And then the thought came-to take the wheel in my hands and quickly turn it into the oncoming traffic and then they would get to see for themselves, front row center, what they drove me to—photograph me to their heart's content slapping up against an immovable force. I imagined clothes, dinner parties, and lovemaking, romantic nights under the moon with you, my dear love, but not this. Not wanting to veer into oncoming traffic at a tremendous speed and everything suddenly, peacefully finally being over. This is where I am, John. This is where my "lack of imagination" has brought me.

Jonathan Fitts

excerpt from

White or the Muskox Play

from

The Best American Short Plays 2011–2012

BON   Dad looked like a zombie. He'd lost a lot of weight. It wasn't like the life drained out of him or anything, you know? It's like he'd already sprung a leak and now we knew what it was. That it was life draining out of him. And we just had to watch. We sat in the car for an hour, and just…*sat* in the AC. I didn't want to cry, you know? Didn't want him to feel bad. Like he needed to protect me. But holy shit. *Holy. Shit.* I couldn't think of anything else. The inside of my head was wallpapered with it. And I looked around…you know, in my head…trying to find other things to focus on. But there weren't. The walls, the windows, they'd all been wallpapered over. Everything else was gone. It had drained out. And I started to get panicky. Almost claustrophobic. I couldn't let it out my eyes, I couldn't let it out my throat. I just had to sit there, with it in my body, pushing from the inside out. And I think Dad had to notice. 'Cause he started fidgeting. And of all things to say, he looked at me and said, "Let's get some ice cream."

Patrick Holland

excerpt from

The Cowboy

from

The Best American
Short Plays 2011–2012

LINDA I'm still figuring this all out. Things at work have gotten so complicated lately. I'm so damn stressed. And it's not just the normal work things. I'm having an affair with my boss. He's married. But we've been seeing each other for a while now.

[*Stopping abruptly. Changing tone, starting over.*]

Let me set this up a little better. I work for an ad agency. Our office is this old three-story mansion that's been converted to condos and offices. Our office shares the top floor with a condo. Business next to pleasure. We just moved into it. There are boxes everywhere. State-of-the-art kitchen, large stainless-steel restaurant fridge (not even plugged in yet), skylights, balcony, view, foosball table, you know.

[*A moment.*]

It was a Saturday. I was coming into work early to get some things done. No one was supposed to be there. It was early in the morning. As I got to the office door, I heard quiet moaning. I put my key in the door.

[*The sounds stop.*]

I walked in and my boss, the man I've been having an affair with, had obviously been up to something, with someone else. I was the "other woman." And now she was. That hurt. That hurt bad. I was angry. [...] He was on the conference table, a favorite spot, naked. But where was she? All I wanted to do was find this "other" "other" woman. He was cheating on me. I wanted to find her. I looked everywhere: closets, under desks in offices, and then, I was standing in the kitchen and I looked out on the balcony. I peered down and saw...two hands gripping a balcony. I was stoned. I was freaked. And now, there was this half-dressed woman hanging from the balcony. I did what I felt. I stepped with purpose on her fingers until she let go. She fell three stories. And I watched. Suddenly, I was an emotional mess. But when she hit the ground it made a sound. [...] Her body broke. But she wasn't dead. She was still breathing. Now, I was really freaked. What had I done?

[*Getting more worked up. More chaotic.*]

I fucking freak. It was like every thing I'd repressed came out at once. She wasn't dead. Shit. Was that good or bad? Shit. Shit. Shit. Shit. I stepped in from the balcony. I needed to fix this. So I went for the nearest and biggest thing I could find. Our fridge, the stainless steel restaurant one…I rolled it across the floor to the edge of the balcony. This thing was heavy, but I was running on adrenaline and emotions. […] I pushed it out on the balcony. Then over the edge. It fell. And it crushed her. Now this might be hard to believe, but the cord caught around my leg. […] and pulled me over the balcony. I hit the fridge and then the pavement. I was dead when I hit the fridge.

Angela C. Hall

excerpt from

Wife Shop

from

The Best American
Short Plays 2011–2012

setting

Includes a sign, "BUMPY'S USED WIFE SHOP." FOXXY has a sign around her neck. The sign reads, "LIKE NEW—FOXXY—STANLEY MODEL BLK 1978." There is a slash through the $10,000 price, and a new price, "50% OFF—$5,000" is listed.

FOXXY   Hi, honey, I made your favorite for dinner…and, look, I even crocheted these new socks…Can't you do anything right? Damn! I'm not gonna put up with this shit! Cook your own goddamn dinner. *She-it!* And cut the goddamn grass already. Do a bitch have to do everything around this motherfucker? I feel like I'm walking through the jungles of Africa.

I've ironed up enough clothes for the entire week, sweetheart. I figure we'll go to church on Sunday, then a nice meal at Olive Garden. Or maybe even a picnic. Oh, that would be lovely, don't you think? Shit, a bitch is tireder than a field slave. Don't just stand there looking at me. Go get me a glass of water or something, motherfucker.

Andrea Sloan Pink

excerpts from

Warner Bros.

from

The Best American
Short Plays 2011–2012

character

TINA twenties. Attractive and smart. Her clothes might be business poetic.

setting

The office. Cheap secretarial furniture and push-button telephones. A large metal Rolodex sits on the table. The other holds a dictionary and porcelain Woodstock pencil cup.

TINA [*Stands alone in office.*] And when I'm driving to work—I mean, I got this crappy car. Totally unromantic. I wanted a Karmann Ghia and instead I ended up with a diesel Rabbit off of auction. Life is like that, you know? Anyway, when I'm driving to work, the sun is always too bright when I come over Barham. I get on the 101 at Highland and then

I've got to do this five-lane switch over to get to the exit, and it's like every time I think I'm going to die on my way to the friggin', pointless, dead-end job, and then I crest over Barham and I'm coming down to the lot, and if the light passes over, I can see it, the wall painters. They'll be there in the early-morning light, under the water tower, dangling off the wall in a harness, and they'll be painting the sunglasses on Tom Cruise's face in super size and I just think, isn't that the coolest thing? Isn't that the coolest thing to see the guy painting the billboard for a movie that's coming out of my studio even though all I'm doing is answering some guy's phone?

[*The phone begins ringing.* TINA *answers.*]

Good morning, John Daniels's office. Please hold. Good morning, John Daniels's office. Please hold for John Daniels.

[TINA *picks up one of the lines.*]

Yes, Mr. Daniels wants to know when his VCR will be repaired. Uh-huh. Uh-huh. I'll tell him. Yes, I tell him next time to take the porn tape out before he brings it in. Mr. Daniels's office, please hold. Mr. Daniels's office, please hold. Drinks at Trumps. Dinner at Morton's. New tires for the Jag.

[TINA *hangs up the phone.*]

We've got to have the story meeting on Rich's boat once a month, so he can write the whole boat off on his taxes. We're sitting down there on deck, and the boat's tied to dock in Marina del Rey, and the wind is whipping and we're all huddled together in the cold, shouting at each other over the gusting wind about the announcements in *Publishers Weekly*.

[*The phone rings again.* TINA *answers.*]

Oh, hi, Duke. No, I can't go out tonight. I have to do John's expenses.

[TINA *hangs up phone and crosses to a window looking out on the lot.*]

What is the value of something old? People look at this lot with its crumbling ghost town and huge soundstages full of used backdrops and they just see the face of it. They don't see the Polish brothers, Hirz, Aaron, Szmul, and Ithzak. Those were their secret names, their hidden names. To the outside world, they were Harry, Albert, Sam, and Jack. They started with a single projector, showing silent films at the Cascade Theater in Pennsylvania. These soundstages were built in 1928. How many hopefuls toiled here, pounding away at a wooden-framed backdrop, dreaming of getting in to the union? This whole place is a ghost town. You feel their spirits moving through the offices, through the old lath and plaster walls. It's the same dust the cowboys rode through when they shot *High Noon*. I don't have a romantic view of it. No, I don't. As far as I'm concerned, hope has a bitter after taste.

• • •

TINA [*On an empty stage.*] When we buried Stu, it was like the air going out of a balloon. Turns out that Stu was Jewish and we all chipped in and got a plot for him at Rose Hills. His mom came out. She had no idea where he'd been living. Rich showed up at the cemetery, the douche bag. That night I went up to the top of Mulholland. When you looked out, you could see Rose Hills in the distance. And in the foreground was the lot. You could tell because it was a big black void surrounded by all those little lights, everybody with their families tucked neatly in their homes. You could barely make out the soundstages in the moon light. The lot. That's what we used to call it. We spent that summer living on the lot. After that, nothing was the same. Lola left for Placerville, and Rich's contract didn't get renewed. Someone else moved into our offices. The desks were thrown onto the scrap heap. One day, years later, after I made my film, I had a meeting on the lot. It was so weird coming back. I had to get a pass to get through the gate. All during the meeting, I never heard a word they said. I couldn't wait to get out of there. All I wanted to do was go back. Afterwards, I didn't go to my car like you're supposed to. I walked down that Western street. I went into the saloon. It was cool and dark. I looked for a crate to pull up but there weren't any. I looked out from the darkness into the bright L.A. light. We didn't all get our day in the sun.

[*Neil Young's "Heart of Gold" comes up as lights fade to black.*]

Crystal Skillman

excerpt from

Rise

from

The Best American
Short Plays 2012–2013

time

Now.

place

A beach in San Francisco.

JOY   This morning I woke up hung over in my own vomit.
The windows were open. My cats escaped. Or I can't find
them. My book has been passed on. That's twenty-four
different publishers. That's twenty-four different agents. And
I don't even like it anymore. It's not me. I'm just trying to be
someone else in it—to sell—sell because I don't know why—I
want to write one story that someone opens and just goes—
that changed me. That changed my life, but I'm not changing
my life. I'm drinking a lot and I tell myself it's the wine that

goes with pasta, but it's too much and Sherry has been falling out of love with me for a long time and I've been watching it happen like a TV show where you know it's happening and Tina, we went through such hell to get her. Do you know I got the book you illustrated with all the monkeys. We sit and we count all the monkeys. All the fucking monkeys and I think I should be good for something. I should be such a good mother. My mother was such a good mother, even though I gave her such shit. Are you going to try to have kids? [...] See, you'll make a good mother. That's what I was thinking when I saw your invitation in the garbage after Sherry took Tina and left. I got off the floor. I got to the airport. I got on a plane. I followed the invitation—had a driver drop me off to Oakland Beach. I'm not like you... I'm shit at writing. When I met you I didn't know what love was. I thought I did. I thought I knew everything. The day we met here. The day you wore your silly pink hat and looked up at the sun, but the sun was me. This gigantic creature of a woman with red hair over you on your beach towel. You said I was in the way of the light. You were drawing the waves. But in them you drew mermaids and creatures of the sea and fantastical things. You said you drew for kids and I told you I made dances for adults. I thought looking at you, drawing, looking away from me that I was seeing beyond something. I'd look at the world and see the beautiful stars and think what I saw was what was. But with you. The stars are a chariot. The waves a home. In my heart. We were always married. Now we are wife and wife. But what a wife is with you changes...and I want it to always change. Like the water. Like us.

I love this poem:

You will remember that leaping stream where sweet aromas rose and trembled, and sometimes a bird, wearing water and slowness, its winter feathers.

You will remember those gifts from the earth, indelible scents, gold clay, weeds in the thicket and crazy roots, magical thorns like swords.

You'll remember the bouquet you picked, shadows and silent water, bouquet like foam-covered stone.

That time was like never, and like always. So we go there, where nothing is waiting; we find everything waiting there.

Edith Freni

excerpt from

Flare

from

The Best American
Short Plays 2012–2013

setting

A two-seater row on a somewhat empty commercial aircraft.
Night flight from New York to Miami.

time

None like the present.

PASSENGER   [*A woman in her thirties. A very bad flier but a
semidecent human being.*] Miami sucks for sports specifically
because of the Marlins! Because of Jeffrey Loria, who is
literally stealing from me. Stealing my money to build this
new stadium, stealing from me to fill it with $140 million
dollars worth of crap free agents who don't know how to win
games and don't need to because as quickly as they come,
they go. They're gone. And nobody cares! The fans don't.

Loria doesn't. The city of Miami doesn't. Everyone's too busy eating Joe's stone crabs and then drinking raw sea turtle eggs at Nikki Beach off the tits of Brazilian volleyball models who balance mangos on their heads while dancing salsa in platform stilettos and triathlon wetsuits. It's absurd. It's a terrible, terrible place to live. To be a fan. Especially when you grew up somewhere like New York. Where people live and die by this shit. In the '90s. In the late '90s. I graduated from high school during Jeter's rookie year. That does something to a person. People live or die. Do you understand me?

[*Beat.*]

Sometimes it's like, it's like the only thing you have to talk about with a person. You meet a stranger and you don't know them but you can talk about baseball.

[*Beat.*]

I think my pill is kicking in.

Janet Allard

Creatures

from

The Best American
Short Plays 2010–2011

characters

A WOMAN

A WEREWOLF (non-speaking)

setting

In the woods. At a drive-in movie. A full moon.

[*At rise:* A WOMAN *and a* WEREWOLF *in a car at a drive-in movie. There is a full moon behind them. The* WOMAN *stares at the* WEREWOLF *in disbelief.*]

WOMAN   So…

Anything else you'd like to tell me?

[*Pause.*]

[*The* WEREWOLF *says nothing.*]

[*He offers her popcorn.*]

No. You can't pretend this is normal, Tom. This is not a normal night at the drive-in anymore.

[*Screams come from the drive-in speakers. A horror film—a B movie.*]

So the monthly business trips to Vegas?

[*He shakes his head.*]

Why didn't you tell me sooner?

[*The* WEREWOLF *is quiet.*]

Did you think I wouldn't find out?

[*Quiet.*]

[*From the movie speakers: "Run! Run for your lives! It's the creature!" (More screams.)*]

When were you planning on telling me? At the alter?

[*Quiet. The* WEREWOLF *eats popcorn.*]

I already knew.

[*The* WEREWOLF *looks at her. Really?*]

I found a strange hair in the bathroom.

[*He goes back to eating popcorn.*]

You are something else, you know that?

I knew it. Somewhere in my I knew this was too good to be true.

So... What now? What does this mean for us, Tom?

[*He shrugs.*]

YOU DON'T KNOW?!

How can you be so nonchalant? It's not like this is going to blow over.

Here's your ring. Here's your goddamn ring back!

[*He stares at her. He offers her popcorn.*]

I don't want popcorn!

[*He howls.*]

You don't scare me.

[*He howls, she howls, he grabs her—*]

[*Movie: romantic music ... maybe a woman's voice—"I'm not afraid of you ... creature!"*]

No! I can't trust you, Tom! I mean...

So what else? What next?

Any other surprises you'd like to spring on me?

[*He lights a cigarette.*]

You smoke?

[*He puts out the cigarette.*]

What else? Bring it on.

[*He shakes his head. This is everything.*]

How am I supposed to believe that?

You hide things—everything—the hair and the teeth…and I never would have known except then the moon—and then you just eat popcorn and—

How can I trust you?

It's *bullshit*, Tom!

I don't keep things from you!

I don't have any secrets!

[WEREWOLF *stares at her.*]

What? I don't.

[*The* WEREWOLF *looks at her.*]

Not like yours.

[*He looks at her.*]

What?

[*She eats popcorn.*]

You know everything about me there is to know. I'm clear. Transparent.

[*He stares at her.*]

What?

What what what?

What?

Why are you looking at me like that?

I'm not keeping anything from you.

[*He sniffs her.*]

I am not hiding—

[*He sniffs harder.*]

I am not hiding any—

Stop sniffing me!

[*He sniffs her like crazy.*]

What are you?!—

No!

[*He pulls a chocolate bar out of her coat. Triumphant.*]

Chocolate! So what?

I was going to share it with you.

[*He goes to take a bite. She grabs it away.*]

Okay! I was hiding it. Hoarding it.

I didn't say I was giving up chocolate forever, just for Lent.

So what? I don't have to share!

[*She devours the entire chocolate bar. He watches. Some sort of melo-dramatic music plays through the movie speakers.*]

It's nothing like I'm keeping something *huge* hidden—like the fact that I'm a *werewolf.* I am happy to eat chocolate out in the open! I love it! I don't care who knows it. And I will not share! And by the way, while we are coming clean—since this is "tell all night"!

[*She pulls a cigarette out of her purse and lights it.*]

I smoke too! I never quit. There. Those are my "shocking secrets." That's all I have to hide.

[*He grabs her hair. It comes off.*]

Alright. It's a wig. So what? I like how it looks.

[*He tries to grab her purse.*]

Stay outta my purse!

[*He gets a text message.*]

[*They both freeze.*]

Is someone texting you?

[*He shrugs.*]

Aren't you going to look?

[*He shrugs.*]

You know, Tom, I think it's good that you revealed this "werewolf business" tonight.

I think it's made us closer. With the nuptials fast approaching we really need to be transparent, get it all out on the table now so it doesn't bite us in the ass, know what I mean? You're a werewolf, I hoard chocolate, we both still smoke. That's it.

Is everything on the table now?

[*He nods.*]

That's everything?

[*He nods.*]

Good.

[*He grabs her purse.*]

Give me back my purse!

[*He holds the purse.*]

Go ahead. Go through it. I don't care.

[*He starts to open the purse—gauging her reaction.*]

You know, Tom, I think trust is a choice. Maybe there are some little things we don't know about each other. We change. We choose. Every day. We choose to trust.

I'm going to choose to trust you. I trust you.

I love you.

[*He smiles.*]

We're missing the movie. Put that down and we can cuddle.

[*She smiles.*]

Do you want more popcorn? I'm dying for some butter on this. Why don't you just run and—

[*He opens the purse. Looks at her to see her reaction. She laughs.*]

Oh, Tom, you're so funny I told you I have nothing to—

[*He sticks his paw into the purse.*]

NO!

[*He rifles through the purse.*]

Hey, asshole—that's my passport!

You have no right to look at my passport!

Yes, I wear bright red lipstick sometimes. So?

I have nothing to—

Yeah, a letter. So what.

Go ahead. Open it.

Yeah, pills. I had a—prescription—they're painkillers for my—

Give me my—

[*He pulls out the ornate box. Stares at it.*]

Put that back—

Put that—

[*He sniffs it.*]

Nothings in that box.

It's just an empty—

You can open it—

Don't—

[*He opens it.*]

[*Screams! On-screen.*]

[*Something in the box glows green. He looks at her in disbelief. She sips her Det Coke.*]

[*She takes the box and puts it back in the purse. She takes the purse. Closes it. And puts it next to her.*]

[*He looks at her. She takes off her wig.*]

Okay. There are some things you need to know about me. I—

[*He shakes his head.*]

It's just that I—

[*He puts his finger to her lips.*]

No, I do need to tell you. I—

[*He puts his finger to her lips. He offers her popcorn.*]

[*She eats popcorn. She starts to cry.*]

[*He puts his paw on her leg.*]

[*Romantic music plays.*]

[*Maybe we hear something from the movie like: "I don't care to return to that world, creature. I'll live where you live. In outer space or at the bottom of the lake. As long as I'm with you." Passionate kissing on the movie screen. Love music. They watch.*]

I'm sorry, I just need to tell you I—

[*She leans over and whispers in his ear.*]

[*He looks at her.*]

And another thing . . .

[*She whispers in his ear.*]

[*He laughs. He whispers in her ear.*]

[*Screams on the screen.*]

[*He puts his arm around her. She puts her head on his chest. The sound of the movie overtakes them.*]

Leslie Ayvazian

Deaf Day

from

The Best American
Short Plays 2001–2002

setting

The set for *Deaf Day* is very simple: a chair. Maybe a footstool.
Perhaps some toys on the ground.

time

Early morning for first scene. Early evening for second scene.

production note

Deaf Day can be performed by a deaf actor or hearing actor, a
woman or a man. The Sign Language must be authentic.

[*A deaf mother talking to a deaf child, who does not appear onstage.
Spoken aloud in English and also in Sign Language.*]

Okay. Ready? Come on!
Sun's up, day's here. Let's go!
Rise and shine.

That means: "Get up and…be happy!" Come on.
Don't ignore me. Look at me! Yes!

We have to practice English. Yes. Today is practice day.
Your teacher said.
So look at me. Look at me!

Put your hearing aids in. Yes! Now!

Good.

Okay.
We're going to the playground.
No, not at Deaf School.
In the park.
Yes, there will be hearing children there.
I don't know if there will be any deaf kids.
You can speak to the hearing children.
Yes, you can. Sure, you can.

Remember the new boy on our street? Roger?
Maybe we'll see new boy Roger and his dog!
You can talk to them. Yes!
And to other kids too.

Yes, you can.
You stand in front of them.
Look directly in their faces.

If they look away, say:
[*No Sign.*] "Could you please repeat that?"
[*No Sign.*] "Could you please repeat that?"

[*With Sign.*] Yes, you can! Say:
[*No Sign.*] "I can't hear you because I'm deaf."

[*Continues aloud and with Sign.*]

Some will laugh.
Some won't laugh.
Talk to the ones who don't laugh.
Come on, honey.
Yes.
Put your shoes on.
Put your shoes on!
I'll put them on you!
Then sit down and put them on!
Sit down!
Now tie your shoes.
Good.
Okay.
Get up.
Get up!
Get up!

Look at me!
Don't turn your head away.
Come on.

OK.

I'll wait . . .

[*She waits. She taps her foot.*]

Hi.

Yes, I'll stay in the park with you, of course.

I'll sit on the closest bench.

You can talk to me whenever you want.

People may watch you.

And some may think: "WOW! Look at this kid!

He knows two languages! How cool!"

Well, some will think, "WOW!"

Some might be stupid.

We will ignore the stupid ones.

Do we feel sorry for the stupid ones?

Nah.

We think they're stupid.

But some people will see how wonderful you are.

And those people will want to talk to you.

So watch their faces.

Read their lips.

If they walk away without telling you where they are going,
    don't be mad.

Hearing people talk with their back to each other.

At those times, wave to me.

We will talk.

And then, we'll come home. Yes.
And you can be quiet for as long as you want to be quiet.
No voices. Quiet.
Quiet.
Okay.

You ready?
Hearing aids, turned on!
Eyes open!
Let's go!

No, we don't have to march.
We can walk slowly!
We can walk real slowly.
And we'll look at each other.
And we'll talk.
In Sign.

We'll talk.
I promise. [*Without Sign.*]

Good. [*Without Sign.*]

[*Lights shift. Lights come up. It is the same day: evening. She speaks aloud and with Sign.*]

Hey.
It's almost time for bed!
Yes, it is!
And you have sleepy eyes.

Yes, yes, yes, you do.
But first...
Look at me, honey.

[*Hits floor for his attention.*]

[*In just Sign.*] Look at me! Good.

[*Continues aloud and with Sign.*]

Let's practice English before we go to bed.
Practice Day is nearly finished.

Watch my face.
Come on, watch.

Let's talk about the park.
No. No Roger! No dog. No.

But the seesaw! Yes!
That girl!
No, we don't know her name.
But you two were perfectly balanced!
You sat in the air at the same time.
That's very special.

But the slide. I know.
They pushed you down the slide.
They wanted you to go faster.
They said: "HEY!...HEY!"

They didn't know that you couldn't hear them.
So they pushed.
They pushed hard. I know.

It surprised you.
And it hurt you. I know.

They pushed you because they were frustrated with you.
But I think you can understand.
Sure you can.
Think about your deaf friends at school
When you want their attention, sometimes you grab them.
Sometimes you hit them.
Sure you do.
Because you want them to look at you.
And you get frustrated. Yes, you do!

So, next time, if the kids are waiting, you go fast!
Okay!
Go fast down that slide.
You kick butt!
Yes!

Then no one will push you.
And no one will laugh.
You need to be fast and quick, quick, quick.
Like a bunny.
Yes.

A fast bunny who kicks butt!
That's you!
Yes!
Right! Jackie Chan!
Okay.

[*Jumps up and does Jackie Chan stance.*]

Jackie Chan! Auhhhhhh!

[*Does tae kwon-do kick.*]

We are Jackie Chan!

[*Another move.*]

But we have sleepy eyes!
Yes.

[*Said in Korean, no Sign.*] Cha-Ryut. Kyung-Net.

[*Bows to him.*] Tae kwon do.

[*Back to Sign and English.*] So get in bed, Jackie Chan!

And maybe, tomorrow we'll go to the planetarium.
Or the zoo?
Maybe the park.
And you can get back in the saddle.

That means: "When you ride a horse and fall off, you need to
    get back on the horse right away."

So you don't feel scared.
Back in the saddle.
Back in the park.
Back on the slide.

Okay?

Okay.

Now sleep, honey.
Sweet dreams.

[*She waves.*]

Sweet dreams.

[*She leaves "his room" and sits. She waits. Then she gets back up and goes to his room. She sees he is still awake, but sleepy. She waves again. She leaves and goes back to her chair. She waits. Then she goes again and checks on him. He's asleep. She returns to her chair and sits. She breathes a sigh of relief. Beat. She notices he has walked into the room. She speaks aloud and in Sign.*]

What's up?
Tomorrow?
Stay home?
All day?
No voices?
Quiet?
I'm thinking.

[*She gets up and sits on the floor.*]

Okay.
Tomorrow.
Quiet.
I promise.
Yes.

[*In just Sign.*] Quiet. Quiet. I promise.

[*In Sign and aloud.*] Good night.

[*In just Sign.*] Good night.

[*She sits watching her son. Lights fade.*]

Susan Miller

excerpts from

It's Our Town, Too

from

The Best American
Short Plays 1992–1993

NOTE:

This monologue may be performed by
either a male or female actor.

STAGE MANAGER   This play is called *It's Our Town, Too*
and all you need to know about who wrote it is she's still here
and constantly wondering.

[*Beat.*]

This first scene is called "An Ordinary Afternoon" and you'll
see two of our main characters, Emily and Elizabeth.

[*A train whistle is heard.*]

It's 4 p.m. in our town. Last night the stars were out like a promise and someone kissed someone they'd never thought of kissing before. Teachers doubted their lessons and Mrs. Kim could be heard singing the overture to *Carousel*. If you were passing through our town, and you happened to stop at the general store for some of Terese Rivera's peach pie, you might be lulled into thinking that people here were small and narrow and wouldn't give a rightful place to the world's concerns. But we're no different from anyone else, trying to grasp the meaning of things. We're mean and lost and fragile and shrewd. We're lonely and aiming too high, bitter and good. We come up thinking the world is sweet but it's every human's experience to meet disappointment.

[*Sound of a bird.*]

Sometimes there's a commotion that sets in over a new possibility. Like the summer three entire families swore they spotted a UFO when it turned out to be Emily Rosen's hopes making themselves known in a burst of light.

[*Beat.*]

Which brings me to Emily and Elizabeth. I suppose there aren't any two people on the planet put together in one place for very long, who don't have their disagreements who don't feel sometimes like maybe they made the worst mistake of their lives or wish the person they thought was so sweet just a few hours before would pack up and leave. There isn't anybody who hasn't looked across the dinner table and thought, I don't know if I love you anymore. And it can drive good people to saying cold words. But it's not really the fact. It's no more true than the first day when you looked at somebody and thought, "She's the one." Thought, "I'm saved." We're just scared is all, every one of us.

[*School bell, sound of young people.*]

Now we're going to go back to the day two of our kind really saw each other for the first time. And knew that there was some future in it.

[*Beat.*]

Oh, this is high school and well, you all remember what that was like. In your heart of hearts aren't you still standing by your locker waiting for that certain one to walk by and maybe, just maybe stop to say your name?

● ● ●

STAGE MANAGER   Excuse me, you're interrupting a wedding.

[*To audience.*]

There's never any lack of trouble for what ought be a person's own business. George's father never spoke to him again after he found out. Emily's mother, well, she kept in touch but wouldn't look Elizabeth in the eye. It's a hard thing when your own turn away. It's a powerful hold they've got on our hearts and minds—Mother. Father. The world is unforgiving enough without the people who brought us up in it taking the other side. So, let's not allow that part of the world in today. Just for a little while, let's give these families a break.

[*Beat.*]

It seems to me we'd all sleep better at night knowing our children had someone decent to worry over them each and every day, each and every time they laid their head down to rest from the day's struggle. What does it matter, all the rest of it?

[*Music starts again.* STAGE MANAGER *turns her back to the audience and toward the couples.*]

I now pronounce you part of the human race that has the good fortune and the daily struggle of being married.

[*Turns her head back to the audience.*]

We wish them all the best, don't we?

[*The lights shift, as the couples move out.* STAGE MANAGER *rearranges the boxes or chairs onstage.*]

Well now, this is the hard part. This last scene, if you haven't already figured it out, is called "The End of Things." Of course, that's only one way of seeing it. Once you've known someone, they never stop being a part of how you look at the world. That goes for the living as well as the dead. And who knows but that we're being watched over somehow or carried out into the eternal universe, by every soul we ever mattered to or mattered to us.

[*Beat.*]

But our sad friends don't know any of this today. So bear with them.

Credits and Permissions

Inquiries concerning rights should be addressed to Zachary Schisgal, zach@theschisgalagency.com.

Schmidt, Kyle John. *St. Matilde's Malady* (excerpt). Copyright © 2012 by Kyle John Schmidt. From *The Best American Short Plays 2010–2011*.

Inquiries concerning rights should be addressed to kylejohnschmidt@yahoo.com.

Silverstein, Shel. *The Devil and Billy Markham.* Copyright © 1991 by Evil Eye, LLC. All rights reserved. Used by permission. From *The Best American Short Plays 1991–1992*. *The Trio* (excerpt). Copyright © 1999 by Shel Silverstein. From *The Best American Short Plays 1997–1998*. And from *The Man-Woman Plays Collection* by Shel Silverstein. Copyright © 2002 by Evil Eye, LLC. All rights reserved. Used by permission.

Inquiries concerning rights should be addressed to Evil Eye, LLC, P.O. Box 5324, Madison, WI 53705-0324.

Skillman, Crystal. *Rise* (excerpt). Copyright © 2013 by Crystal Skillman. From *The Best American Short Plays 2012–2013*.

Inquiries concerning rights should be addressed to crystalskillman@gmail.com and Amy Wagner, Abrams Agency, amy.wagner@abramsartny.com.

Soderberg, Douglas. *The Root of Chaos* (excerpt). Copyright © 1984 by Douglas Soderberg. From *The Best American Short Plays 1986*.

Inquiries concerning rights should be addressed to
soderdou@att.net.

Soland, Lisa. *Spatial Disorientation* (excerpts). Copyright © 2013
by Lisa Soland. From *The Best American Short Plays
2012–2013*.

Inquiries concerning rights should be addressed to
lisasoland@aol.com.

Thelen, Lawrence. *Ichabod Crane Tells All*. Copyright © 2013
by Lawrence Thelen. From *The Best American Short Plays
2011–2012*.

Inquiries concerning rights should be addressed to
lawrence.thelen@gmail.com or care of the Dramatists
Guild, New York.

van Itallie, Jean-Claude, and Joseph Chaikin, *Struck Dumb*.
Copyright © 1992 by Jean-Claude van Itallie and Joseph
Chaikin. From *The Best American Short Plays
1991–1992*.

Inquiries concerning rights should be addressed to
jcvani@hughes.net.

Wellman, Mac. *The Sandalwood Box* (excerpts). Copyright ©
1995–1996 by Mac Wellman. From *The Best American
Short Plays 1995–1996*.

Inquiries concerning rights should be addressed to
Buddy Thomas, ICM Talent, bthomas@iocmtalent.com.

Other Monologue and Scene Books
Available from Applause Books & Limelight Editions